Contents

#TRANSGENDER

WHAT IS GENDER?

Gender usually refers to whether you are a boy or a girl. Your gender affects many things, from your name to what others expect from you.

Boy or girl?

Each one of us has a sense of who we are. We know what our favourite food is, the music we like, our best lessons at school, our closest friends and what our secret daydreams and goals are. This is all part of our identity and what makes us who we are. A big part of your identity is whether you see yourself as a boy or a girl or neither – this is your gender identity. How you identify affects everything in your life, from how society sees you, to the way you do your hair, the clothes you wear and the things you choose to do.

It's a ...

Our gender is based on whether we are born with a penis or a vagina. Depending on which we have, we are called a boy or a girl. This is known as our assigned gender identity, which is given to us at birth.

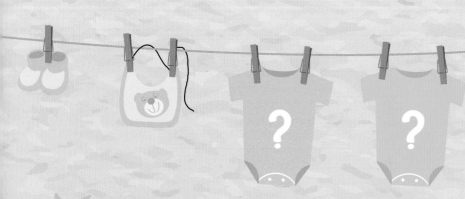

UNDERSTANDING TRANSGENDER

HONOR HEAD

W

Franklin Watts
Published in paperback in Great Britain in 2019 by The Watts Publishing Group

Credits:
Series Editor: Jean Coppendale
Series Designer: Lorraine Inglis
Consultant: Dr Claudia Zitz, The Tavistock and Portman Clinic

With many thanks to Dan for his story on pages 24–27, and in memory of his Aunt Mae
who was such an inspiration.

Picture credits:
Every attempt has been made to clear copyright. Should there be any inadvertent omission please apply
to the publisher for rectification.
t = top, b = bottom, l = left, r = right, m = middle
Cover: © Shutterstock/Trifonenkolvan
All images listed here are © of Shutterstock and: 4b hancik; 6-7 Incombile; 8 AVABitter, 9t mlorenz;
10 Lorelyn Medina; 12-13 Michael D Brown; 14 whiteisthecolour; 15b Helga Esteb; 18 sitting figure
Kakigori Studio, changing room Lorelyn Medina, 19door GraphicsRF; 20t Beatriz Gascon J;
24 earphones stockhype; 28-29 background, kampolz, birds, Mrs. Opossum.

Note to parents and teachers: Every effort has been made by the Publishers to ensure that these websites are
suitable for children, that they are of the highest educational value, and that they contain no inappropriate or
offensive material. However, because of the nature of the Internet, it is impossible to guarantee that the contents
of these sites will not be altered. We strongly advise that Internet access is supervised by a responsible adult.

ISBN 978 1 4451 5565 4
Printed in Dubai

Franklin Watts
An imprint of
Hachette Children's Group
Part of The Watts Publishing Group
Carmelite House
50 Victoria Embankment
London EC4Y 0DZ

An Hachette UK Company
www.hachette.co.uk

www.franklinwatts.co.uk

No right or wrong way

Most families and societies have certain expectations of how people should behave based on their gender. Families generally expect girls to want to play with dolls, wear dresses and like dancing, which are seen as being feminine, and boys to enjoy toy cars and rough and tumble games, which is seen as being masculine. But there is no right or wrong way that girls and boys should behave because of their gender.

Some young girls are tomboys and like climbing trees, while some young boys like dressing up. But there can be peer pressure and expectations from family, school and the community to conform to 'norms', to behave as girls are expected to behave and boys are expected to behave.

What we do as **children** is all part of getting to know ourselves and the *world* around us.

TALKBACK!

Look out for the TALKBACK boxes. This is where you and your friends, family or classmates can discuss two sides of an argument. There are no right or wrong answers, but you might be surprised at the conclusions you come to.

What is transgender?

Transgender or trans describes people who feel that their body doesn't match the gender they believe they are.

Gender identity

Transgender is a general term to describe people who don't feel they identify with the gender they were given at birth. For example, a trans boy given or assigned the female gender at birth may feel odd behaving in a way that a girl is expected to behave: to dress as a girl, have a girl's name or be referred to as 'she' and 'her'. She doesn't feel like a girl inside and rejects girly things, such as sparkly pink stuff, long hair and dolls. She may even feel that she is living a lie and that people expect the wrong things from her.

Body dysphoria

Body dysphoria or gender dysphoria is when a person feels deeply unhappy with the body they have because it is the wrong gender. This feeling of being in the wrong body can start from about the age of 2 or 3, but can happen at any age into adulthood. Puberty can be an especially hard time for trans young people. They can become distressed with their own body as it starts to change, and for girls when their periods begin (see page 20).

This is not me!

For many young people being transgender can cause them a lot of stress and unhappiness. They can feel under pressure from family and society to behave in a way that is completely wrong for them. Many children find it hard to express what the problem is, especially when they may not even understand it themselves. They become frustrated and confused and can feel guilty and ashamed and fearful that there is something terribly wrong with them.

Not so simple

Some trans people are binary. This means that they want to change the gender they were assigned at birth to the opposite gender. Gender fluid, gender non-binary, pangender and genderqueer describe people who feel they are neither male nor female, or feel one and then the other; they believe there are many genders. For some people, gender is something that can shift and change like our moods and emotions.

7

TRANS IS NOT LGB!

Being transgender is not the same as being gay, lesbian or bisexual, but transgender and LGB can overlap.

The same but different

Being transgender is about who a person is, how they identify themselves and how they want to live their life. Being LGB is about sexual attraction and romantic feelings towards another person. Many LGB people are happy with the sex they were born with, they are just attracted to people of the same sex. A gay male will see himself as a man who is attracted to other men, and a gay female as a woman attracted to other women. Bisexual people are attracted to both men and women.

Trans and being LGB

Transgender people can be lesbian, gay or bisexual, so a boy who has become a girl who finds other girls attractive may identify herself as a lesbian. Sexual feelings can be very confusing for young transgender people. Some know straight away whether they prefer to be with people of their own (chosen) sex or the opposite sex, but some may be attracted to people of the same sex, or to both sexes, and some may find their feelings change as they get older.

Confused!

Some young transgender people may go through a time when they believe they are LGB. This is because they might be attracted to a person of the same sex. But as they come to understand their situation more, they realise they are attracted to that person as their preferred gender, not as their birth gender. It can be very confusing and you should talk to a helpline or a counsellor if you have any concerns about the way you feel.

Gender is how we feel about ourselves, *sexuality* is how we feel about other people.

Dress code

Some LGB people may enjoy dressing up as the opposite sex but still want to keep their assigned birth gender.

- Drag queens are men who like being men but enjoy dressing up in women's clothes. They usually do so as a form of public entertainment.

- Drag kings are women who like being women but also dress and behave as men, again usually as entertainment.

- Transvestites are usually men who sometimes enjoy dressing in women's clothes.

Drag queens, drag kings and transvestites might be transgender, lesbian, gay, bisexual or heterosexual.

BEING ME

The path to finding their preferred self is different for each transgender person and it can be a long and challenging journey.

Transitioning

Most transgender people want to live their lives as the gender they feel they really are, so they may decide to change from a girl to a boy or a boy to a girl or become gender fluid. This change is called transitioning. It's a huge decision to make and is one that affects family, friends and school life. For many the journey will begin by social transitioning – changing their name to their preferred gender, so Belinda might become Billy and David become Daisy, dressing in the way of their preferred gender and restyling their hair. Trans people will want everyone to use the preferred pronouns, he/him or she/her if they are binary (transitioning from one gender to another), or they/them or ze/zir if they are gender fluid.

Deciding when

When to socially transition depends on the child and their family. A child at primary school might wait until they go to secondary school; some children will wait until they are teens or adults before making any obvious changes. Some may be known as their preferred identity at home with close family and friends, but carry on as their birth identity with the rest of their friends and at school until they feel ready to make the situation public knowledge (see page 14).

Body issues

Trans people with body dysphoria may decide to have some form of surgery so that their body matches their preferred gender. This will help them feel more comfortable with their body. Surgery is usually done when the trans person is an adult and can be a very emotional step for the transgender person and their family and friends. Some trans people can accept the body they have, even though they may dress like their preferred gender or as both genders.

Options

As transgender becomes more understood and accepted by society, so more children are understanding what is happening to them and can talk about their feelings. There are now many organisations that will give children and families the support they need to transition and to help them consider all their options (see page 31).

FAMILY SUPPORT

Young trans people need a lot of support from family and friends when they are transitioning, and the family needs support, as well.

Mixed feelings

When a person starts to transition it can be very distressing for the parents, grandparents and other close family who may feel that they are 'losing' a child and be very sad. Some parents may feel that the child has become transgender because of something they've done. This is not true. Transgender is not caused by anything anyone has done. And even though there may be a sense of loss to begin with, over time most families will be happy that their child is doing what is important for their personal happiness and growth, and will usually support them as much as they can.

Siblings

Siblings might be confused about what is happening to their brother or sister. They might miss their sibling and feel jealous or left out if the transgender child gets a lot of extra attention from the family. If they go to the same school as their trans sibling, they might be bullied or teased. But a sibling can be a strong support for a trans child when they understand what is going on.

Friends

Some friends might feel that they don't share the same interests with the trans person any more. Some might turn nasty or be told to stay away from the trans friend by their family. This is hurtful. Supportive friends are important to help trans people face the challenges ahead.

Family support

For the transitioning child there is usually a sense of relief that at last they can be their preferred selves with their family. However, some families or family members may find it hard to accept the changes for many reasons. Look for local trans groups or LGBT groups for families and young people where everyone can discuss their concerns with others who have been through the same experiences.

TALKBACK!

How do you think you would react if your best friend said they were transgender?

It would be like getting to know them all over again. I may not like the 'new' friend. It would be too weird.

No problem! Deep down my friend is the same ... all that has changed is how the friend looks so I'd have to get used to that.

Transitioning at school

When and how a person decides to transition at school is entirely up to them.

School privacy

There are no rules about when a person can or should start to transition at school and some trans students decide to never come out at school. For some students keeping their transgender identity private can make them feel safer and it is one less thing to worry about. For others it may create more worry and stress having to switch identities for school and it can make them feel anxious about being 'found out'. Often the decision is made as a family together with the school, as it will affect everyone, including siblings who may go to the same school.

> Discuss these reasons why a student should or should not tell those at school or outside the family that they are trans.

I'll lose my friends if they think I'm not one of them any more.

Telling people will help others who are a minority to come out.

People will talk behind my back if they know. I'll be an outcast.

I'd feel really guilty about keeping such a big secret from my family and friends.

Ideas for coming out

For those who do decide to come out at school, here are some ideas.

- ✓ Talk to a teacher at school about giving a talk on transgender at assembly.
- ✓ Ask a teacher to speak to the class about transgender with you, which is not quite so scary!
- ✓ Tell your close friends and then ask them to tell others.

Whatever the trans person decides to do, true friends will understand their concerns and respect their decisions. Other students might be jealous that the transgender student is getting special attention or privileges, such as using the staff toilet, and use this as an excuse for bullying. But most trans people want to be accepted just like everyone else and to get on with their life feeling safe and happy.

> *There's a gender in your brain and a gender in your body. For 99 percent of people, those things are in alignment. For transgender people, they're mismatched. That's all it is.*
>
> Chaz Bono (b. 1969), US musician and actor

SCHOOL POLICY

Most schools now have guidelines to help transitioning children feel safe and respected.

Practical stuff

Most schools will offer lots of support to a transitioning student. The process will usually start with the family having a meeting with staff to discuss the issues. Teachers and schoolmates should start to call the trans person by their new, chosen name and use their preferred pronoun, such as her or him or they/zir if the person is gender fluid. Some schools have a gender neutral uniform policy, so a girl can wear trousers and a boy a skirt, but if not, uniform options can be discussed with the school. Other practical issues include which toilets and changing rooms to use and which PE class to go to if they are based on 'boys' or 'girls'. All of these issues will vary from school to school but there should be acceptable options available.

Clothing for classes, such as swimming or water-based sports, can be an issue. Perhaps your school could adopt a sports kit that includes baggy shorts or skirted swimsuits and vests that lots of kids might be more comfortable wearing, for all sorts of different reasons.

Talk to teachers

Kids transitioning who have concerns or who are being bullied should talk to their teachers. It is the school's responsibility to provide a safe learning environment, but this is such a new situation that the school may get it wrong or not have the facilities needed. Often trans students have to use the staff toilets and changing rooms, which can make them feel even more different and isolated from their peers and cause teasing. Suggest that the disabled toilet be called the 'unisex', 'accessible' or 'larger' toilet.

TALKBACK!

Why is it important to call a trans person by their chosen name?

This name represents the person they really feel they are. Your name is a big part of your identity.

A name is just a word. You're still the same person, whatever you're called.

The right name

For a trans student, being called by their preferred name is very important to them. Teachers and pupils should use their new chosen name but it may not appear on exam papers. Only the student's legal birth name is used on exam papers unless the name has been changed by deed poll. It can be upsetting for a trans student to have to acknowledge a name they don't believe is theirs, but it is important to focus on the exam and not let the use of a birth name stop anyone doing the best they can.

BULLYING and discrimination

No one should ever have to put up with bullying or discrimination because of the way they live their life.

Changing challenge

Using the changing rooms and toilets of their birth gender may make a trans person feel vulnerable and embarrassed. There are guidelines on how schools should treat these issues, so trans students should speak to a PE teacher or other trusted teacher if they feel unsafe, anxious or are being bullied in the changing room or during games. If other students feel uneasy having a trans schoolmate in their changing room or toilet, talk to a supportive teacher about the concerns. Talk through the issues and see what can be done to make everyone feel comfortable. The school cannot discriminate against a person because they are transgender. If a person feels they are being left out of anything because they are trans, there is no need to feel ashamed or suffer in silence ... talk to the school or a trusted adult.

Sticking together

Siblings of transgender children, especially those who attend the same school or one nearby, and even friends, might be victims of bullying or teasing. This can be tough, and the trans person really needs support, and the more people who stand up against bullying, prejudice and discrimination, the more likely it is to stop. If you can, ask the bullies why they're behaving the way they are – usually it is through ignorance or fear or are attitudes they've picked up from other people.

Get creative

Write and perform a play about gender diversity. Instead of splitting groups into boys and girls try colours or animals. Set up a safety zone for those being bullied. Organise debates using some of the issues discussed in this book. Maybe get a speaker from an LGBT group to give an assembly or workshop (see page 31).

Bully-free zone

Make your school a bully-free zone and keep it a safe place for everyone. Don't 'like' hurtful remarks online or join in with jokes or teasing. Don't deliberately call a trans person the wrong pronoun or birth name. This can be very hurtful to the trans person who wants to be accepted as their preferred identity. If a trans student or anyone is being bullied, go with them to report it or stand by them – it can be very hard to fight back when you are feeling scared and alone.

PUBERTY – HELP!

Puberty is difficult for all young people but especially for many trans children and their families. They will often have to make some life-changing decisions.

Body change

At puberty our bodies grow and develop into more masculine or more feminine shapes depending on our sex. This is because hormones are released into the body that trigger a series of changes.

For girls this means:
▶ breasts start to grow
▶ hips fill to create a more womanly shape
▶ periods start.

For boys this means:
▶ facial hair starts to grow
▶ muscles develop
▶ voice gets deeper
▶ Adam's apple begins to grow.

Oh, no!

For trans children puberty can be more challenging than for most. Suddenly their body is becoming something hateful and alien. Characteristics such as breasts, hips, muscles and body hair, that make us look more feminine or masculine, for a trans person mean that they are becoming the person they don't want to be. This can contribute to feelings of depression, isolation and guilt and, for some, extreme behaviour such as self-harming and even feelings of suicide.

Professional advice

At puberty the family of a trans child may decide to visit a gender clinic for advice from professional counsellors. The child may be offered puberty-suppressing drugs. These are drugs that can put puberty 'on hold' while the child has counselling and talks through their options for the future.

Changing mind

Many trans children change their mind about transitioning when they reach puberty. They might still cross-dress now and again, or they might realise they are gender fluid. Whatever stage they have reached, they have the right to change their mind about how they see themselves and their future and shouldn't feel guilty about it.

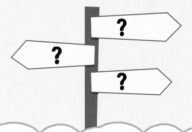

People might be curious about the physical changes a trans person might be going through. Do you have the right to ask them personal questions about their body?

If they talk about what's happening it helps everyone to understand a bit more.

Respect their privacy. They may not want to discuss it or think they are different from everyone else.

Would you like to answer personal questions about your private parts?

I think it's being nosey! Why should they talk about private matters to everyone?

Transitioning – the journey

The ultimate aim for some transgender kids will be to transition completely to their preferred gender.

Social transitioning

For most people the first stage of changing gender is social transitioning. This includes being called by a name and pronouns appropriate to their preferred gender, changing hairstyle and wearing different clothes. Some people begin the social transition at home first, or with close friends they trust, then socially transition at school or work and in the wider community. Some people might never socially transition outside their home; others might not socially transition at all if they feel it is not right for them or if they may be in danger from or by rejected from their home or community.

Hormone treatment

Some trans people might decide to begin a physical transition; that is, actually changing their body. This includes hormone treatment and can be started in the early stages of puberty. Some hormone treatments help to stop puberty and can be reversed later. Other hormone treatments are not reversible. Before taking any treatment it is important for trans people to have advice from professionals who can explain what is involved. F2M (female to male) might chest bind to hide their growing breasts. M2F (male to female) might have laser treatment to permanently remove unwanted facial hair.

Surgery

The surgery a trans person decides to have will vary enormously from one person to another. Only adults over the age of 18 are legally allowed surgery in most countries. Above waist or top surgery for F2M means having their breasts removed. Below waist or bottom surgeries means creating a vagina for M2F and a penis for F2M. Many trans people never have below waist or genital surgery and still live their life completely as their preferred gender. Below waist surgeries can take a long time.

Not alone

Transgender clinics can offer medical advice, treatment and psychological support to trans people and their families, and there are many other charities and organisations that can provide counselling and emotional support. No young person needs to feel that this is a journey they have to make alone. It is essential to learn as much as possible about the various procedures and discuss them with trained professionals and family before making major decisions that can't be changed.

For each person, the *journey* to their preferred self will be very **different**.

Dan's story

Dan was assigned female at birth. He is now 17 and at school doing exams and transitioning to male. This is Dan's story...

> " I have always been unhappy being a girl. When I was in primary school all of my friends were boys and I'd love joining in with all of their games but because I was a girl they wouldn't let me play with them or I would be given a female role like a nurse, which made me very angry. Everyone my age knew I was different and didn't fit in so I was often alone, reading by myself. I experienced really severe bullying of all kinds in primary school but at that age no one took it seriously as [adults] didn't believe that a child could be that nasty. I was bullied continuously through school but it had always been the norm for me so it never bothered me.

I want to be me!

I was always pushed towards 'girly' things or told I couldn't do something because it was for boys or unladylike. I wanted to join the Scouts but was told that girls couldn't go because Brownies was for girls and Scouts was still seen as just for boys. Brownies was my idea of hell. I just wanted to be me.

I wanted the same things as my younger brother [now aged 15] but rarely got the same; even when we did, mine was always **pink** because I was the **girl** and everything had to be **gendered**.

I considered myself a tomboy, which at the time was the closest label I had to explain how I felt, but always felt frustrated because I knew it didn't quite fit. I just didn't have the language to put a name to it.

I started to experiment with my gender when I was about 11 or 12 - before that I had no idea I even had a choice, I just thought that girls had to be one way and boys another. I started to dress as a boy by tucking my long hair into a hat and wearing plaid shirts done all the way up with baggy trousers and army uniform. Doing this felt like I was closer to being me.

I decided to do more **research** to figure myself out and came across **transgender**: it was like everything clicked into place and finally made *sense* because I'd found the **word** I had been looking for all those years.

Torture!

I began to feel really bad when I hit puberty. There were expectations to like boys and wear make-up and bras and at this point some girls were even getting excited about periods. I felt like I had been dropped on a completely different planet. I had no idea that hormone blockers existed at this time so I went through puberty, hating every second of it. Periods are the worst part of it - to me that time of the month feels like medieval torture. I genuinely feel I am male so I forget that it happens to me, which makes it all the more painful when it inevitably rolls back around. By the time I was 13 I felt like tearing my own skin off, as if the real me was trapped underneath.

Coming out

When I came out I told my friends first, as they were the people who were most accepting of me and knew me best. I never got any negativity from them as the more I explained how I felt, the more it made sense to them too. They started calling me by my preferred name and pronouns, and defended me whenever anyone else picked on me or refused to accept it.

School time

I was 12 or 13 when I had a meeting with my tutor and the head of my year at school and explained what I was experiencing. The teachers were very understanding and the school changed my name to Dan on the register and ensured everyone used it along with male pronouns. Uniform wasn't a problem because the school has no strict guidelines for what boys/girls wear as long as it's within the rules. My family had no idea this was happening.

For a while I didn't do PE at all because the school felt they couldn't put me with the boys in case they rejected me like the girls did. The next year the school changed PE to being mixed gender so that I could take part without anyone having to worry. There was a similar situation with toilets and changing rooms so I had to use the disabled toilets in both scenarios.

Telling Mum and Dad

My parents didn't find out until I'd already been living as male for a whole year. I told them as I knew I would need their help and understanding if I was going to get my name changed [legally] or receive any kind of treatment. My family struggled to accept it and still do a lot of the time, but they know that I am absolutely certain of my [male] identity.

New hair!

I started to socially transition when I was about 12 or 13. I already had a very masculine wardrobe so I didn't have to change a lot. The only major difference was cutting off my hair. I had to be sneaky about it as I wasn't out to my parents yet; I told them I wanted short hair because my hair was too high maintenance. It took quite a few months of nagging to convince my mum to let me do it, but I guess she saw that I was so determined that if she didn't agree to it I'd try cutting it myself anyway.

I was so excited at every major change I underwent and would smile for days after - I don't think I've ever been as happy as I was when I first stood in front of a mirror with short hair, flat chest [Dan uses a chest binder] and men's clothes on for the first time. It is the best feeling in the world - freedom.

But I still don't recognise my body underneath the clothes - it's like my head has been stitched onto a stranger's body. I feel like a real-life version of Frankenstein's monster.

I've wanted **hormone** treatment and top *surgery* since I first found out about it. I've never once felt uncertain about it. I'm just *waiting* for it to happen.

SO, TO RECAP...

This is a recap of the issues we have looked at in this book. They are presented as ideas to discuss. Talking things through can help us to understand ourselves and others a little better and why we react in the way we do in certain situations and to different people.

Gender identity

Gender is about how we identify ourselves. Most of us think of ourselves as being a boy or a girl. What do you think being a boy means? And what does being a girl mean? What does it mean to be feminine and to be masculine? Can a person be masculine and feminine? Does being feminine and masculine mean different things in different cultures? Do our ideas of what it means to be a boy or a girl change as we get older?

Support and respect

Transgender people often feel isolated and alone, ashamed and anxious about what is happening to them. How can you best support someone who is transgender? What can the school do to support them? What might be difficult issues for transgender students at school?

Community support

Some communities still find it very difficult to support transgender people. This can be very hurtful and sometimes dangerous for trans people. What are some things young people can do if they don't have the support of their family and community? Why do you think it is difficult for some families and communities to support young trans people?

Feeling wrong

Transgender people feel that they are being expected to live as the wrong gender. Try to imagine that you wake up one morning and everyone thinks you are the opposite gender to the one you are, they call you by another name and expect you to wear different clothes and behave differently. How would you feel? Would it be scary? How could you explain to your family and friends that they are making a mistake? What do you think the worst things would be about being the wrong gender?

Glossary

assigned gender identity the gender identity, usually boy or girl, that a baby is given at birth

binary formed of or involving two things; with reference to transgender, boy and girl

bisexual someone who is sexually attracted to both men and women

chest bind when someone wears a tight band across their breasts to look flat-chested

deed poll the way to legally change your name

discrimination unfair treatment of someone based on their colour, religion, sex, age, etc.

dysphoria to feel deeply unhappy, uncomfortable and distressed about something

community the place or a group that you are part of and share things with such as attitude, family, beliefs and values

gay homosexual men and more generally all homosexual people

gender identity your own identity as a male, female, both or neither

gender fluid a person who feels they are a blend of male and female

genitals a person's reproductive organs, such as penis and testicles in a male and vagina and womb in a female

heterosexual a person who is sexually attracted to people of the opposite sex

hormone blockers medication that can block the release of the hormones testosterone (male) and oestrogen (female) into the body, to stop puberty

hormones chemicals produced by the body to help it grow and keep it working properly

lesbian a woman who is sexually attracted to other women

LGB letters that stand for lesbian, gay and bisexual

peer pressure when you feel you have to do something you don't want to because your friends or classmates are doing it

periods a girl's monthly menstrual cycle when blood and other substances lining the womb are discharged from the body through the vagina

prejudice an unfair or unjust opinion which is not based on knowledge or experience

pronouns words used to describe a person such as him/her and she/he

puberty the age or time when hormones released into your body cause it to begin to develop and change into an adult body.

sibling a brother or sister

testicles (also called testes) two round organs behind the penis that make sperm in men

transgender a person whose personal identity and gender does not match the one given to them at birth

transitioning changing from one gender to another

Further information

Note to parents and teachers: every effort has been made by the Publishers to ensure that these websites are suitable for children, that they are of the highest educational value and that they contain no inappropriate or offensive material. However, because of the nature of the Internet, it is impossible to guarantee that the contents of these sites will not be altered. We strongly advise that Internet access is supervised by a responsible adult.

WEBSITES AND HELPLINES

If you feel overwhelmed by any of the issues you've read about in this book or need advice, check out a website or call a helpline and talk to someone who will understand.

http://gids.nhs.uk/young-people
The Gender Identity Development Service, part of the Tavistock and Portman Clinic. Advises and counsels families and young people.

http://genderedintelligence.co.uk
Free downloadable pdfs, school visits, creative workshops, activities and groups to bring trans young people together. Support for young trans people by trans people.

www.mermaidsuk.org.uk
Advice, counselling and support for young trans people and their families. School training supplied. Helpline: 0344 334 0550 (charged).

www.nhs.uk/conditions/Gender-dysphoria
Explains gender dysphoria, has video real-life stories, and further useful links.

www.sandyford.org
NHS service in Scotland.

www.supportline.org.uk
A charity giving emotional support to children and young people.

For readers in Australia and New Zealand

www.transcendsupport.com.au
Online support network and information hub for transgender children and their families.

https://gendercentre.org.au/
Counselling, information, videos, support groups, education services and much more for the transgender community.

www.opendoors.net.au/changeling-aspects/
A list of transgender support groups in Australia and New Zealand.

www.healthdirect.gov.au/partners/kids-helpline
A helpline for young people giving advice, counselling and support.

www.kidsline.org.nz
Helpline run by young volunteers to help kids and teens deal with troubling issues and problems.

Books and other stuff

www.intercomtrust.org.uk/item/55
A free guide for schools on transgender issues.

Can I tell you about gender diversity? by C.J. Atkinson, Jessica Kingsley Publishers, 2017. An introduction to gender dysphoria told through the make-believe story of Kit aged 12, followed by a guide for children, parents and professionals.

Index

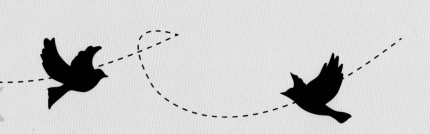

SPECTATOR SAFETY

Bill Croft

DERBY college
LEARNING RESOURCE
CENTRE

www.pearsonschoolsandfe.co.uk

✓ Free online support
✓ Useful weblinks
✓ 24 hour online ordering

0845 630 44 44

Heinemann

Part of Pearson

Heinemann is an imprint of Pearson Education Limited, Edinburgh Gate, Harlow, Essex, CM20 2JE.

www.pearsonschoolsandfecolleges.co.uk

Heinemann is a registered trademark of Pearson Education Limited

Text © Pearson Education Limited 2011
Edited by Davina Thackara
Designed by Lorraine Inglis
Typeset by Phoenix Photosetting, Chatham, Kent
Illustrated by Phoenix Photosetting and kja-artists.com
Original illustrations © Pearson Education Limited 2011
Front cover photograph © www.imagesource.com

The right of Bill Croft to be identified as author of this work has been asserted by him in accordance with the Copyright, Designs and Patents Act 1988.

First published 2011

14 13 12 11 10
10 9 8 7 6 5 4 3 2 1

British Library Cataloguing in Publication Data
A catalogue record for this book is available from the British Library

ISBN 978 0 435 04737 5

Printed in the UK by Scotprint

There are links to relevant websites in this book. In order to ensure that the links are up to date and that the links work we have made the links available on www.pearsonhotlinks.co.uk. Search for this title NVQ Spectator Safety or ISBN 97804 35047375.

Contents

Acknowledgements and Credits

The publisher would like to thank the following for their kind permission to reproduce their photographs:

(Key: b-bottom; c-centre; l-left; r-right; t-top)

Alamy Images: Adrian Sherratt 121, 144, Charles Stirling 40, Gari Wyn Williams 24, Image 66, Neil McAllister 68, Neil Tingle 53, Robert Noyes 151, Timothy Aikman 35, Toby Allen 8; **Corbis:** Matthew Ashton / AMA 100, Michele Constantini 89, moodboard 85; **Fotolia.com:** benoit sarasin 118, David Davis 83, Paul Hill 33; **Getty Images:** 79, Ben Edwards 82t, Bongarts 22, Dennis Doyle 41, John Rowley 103, 156, Lori Adamski Peek 135, Mike Flokis 46, Morne de Klerk 63, Oli Scarff 139, Steve Taylor 133; **Masterfile UK Ltd:** Paul Wright 130; **Pearson Education Ltd:** David Sanderson 23/1, 23/2, 23/3, 23/6, 23/8; Roddy Paine 6, 49; Stuart Cox 1, 2, 37, 43, 109, 110, 124, 134; **Photolibrary.com:** Alex Hinds 74, Godong 7, Jochen Tack 58; **Press Association Images:** Fiona Hanson / PA Archive 154, Mike Egerton / EMPICS Sport 82b, Neal Simpson / EMPICS Sport 143, Nigel French / EMPICS Sport 115; **Rex Features:** Back Page Images 70, Barry Wilkinson 27, Charles Knight 105, Richard Gardner 146, Sonny Meddle 137; **Select Security Group Ltd:** 113; **Showsec:** 19, 75, 91, 145; **Shutterstock.com:** absolute-india 159, c. 23/9, humpkin 23/5, jcjgphotography 127, Jess Yu 111, Luis Santos 12, MARKABOND 23/4, Naturaldigital 23/7, Yuri Arcurs 61

All other images © Pearson Education

Picture research by: Sally Cole

The following public sector information is licensed under the Open Government Licence v1.0.

- p. 29 extract from Health & Safety at Work Act, 1974
- p. 103 extract from Criminal Law Act, 1967 (sec 3)
- pp. 104–105 Guide to Safety at Sports Grounds

Every effort has been made to trace the copyright holders and we apologise in advance for any unintentional omissions. We would be pleased to insert the appropriate acknowledgement in any subsequent edition of this publication.

About the author

Bill Croft was an operational police officer for 30 years, completing his career as a chief inspector heading crime prevention for West Midlands Police, (the UK's second largest police force) and was later seconded to the Home Office Crime Reduction College responsible for consulting with outside organisations and the police service. Since retiring from the police, Bill has had a number of years of direct experience within the security industry; since 1996 he has managed a successful company as a security consultant, training provider and external verifier for NVQ's including Spectator Safety and Event Management.

Bill has worked with national awarding bodies, the Office of the Deputy Prime Minister, The Security Company based in the Netherlands (Europe's largest event company), Showsec International, Wembley Stadium, and many other companies within the security and event industries. Bill is an experienced National Awarding Body External Verifier, International External Verifier and Lead Verifier for Spectator Safety, Security Guarding, PTLLS, Community Safety, Custodial Care, and a number of security-related subjects including Close Protection, Spectator Safety, Investigations, Public Services, Drug Awareness, Equality and Diversity Custodial Care and Occupational Health and Safety at over forty centres in England and Wales. Bill is also a qualified National Security Inspector, a Quality Auditor and Centre Approval Advisor. Bill has also written a number of articles and qualifications in Personal Safety at Work, Terrorism Awareness, CCTV, Event Stewarding/Spectator Safety, and Accredited Persons and has been involved in working parties developing security-related qualifications at Skills for Security. He is also contracted by awarding bodies to write qualifications.

Introduction

NVQ Level 2 Spectator Safety and the Award in Understanding Stewarding at Spectator Events

This is an extremely exciting time for the events industry, and therefore for anyone undertaking a qualification in spectator safety. In the next few years there are plenty of high-profile international sporting events to look forward to, including the 2012 London Olympic and Paralympic Games and the 2015 Rugby World Cup in Twickenham.

Alongside these major events, there are many other events of all sizes and catering for all interests taking place. For example, the following will all require event stewards:

- a multitude of annual music festivals, ranging from the large ones such as Glastonbury, V, and Latitude, to smaller ones such as Truck in Steventon, Kendal Calling in Keswick and Summer Sundae in Leicester.
- exhibitions, such as Grand Designs Live at Birmingham NEC and the UK Wedding Show at Manchester Central
- outdoor events, such as one-off carnivals and proms in parks
- gigs and various sporting events that take place on a weekly basis.

There has never been a better time to study for a qualification in spectator safety. Getting involved in the events industry and undertaking this qualification can provide you with exciting opportunities and a chance to widen your skills.

This candidate handbook has been written by an experienced author who understands how important it is to develop diverse skills in order to succeed in this industry. It will help you to develop your role as an events steward, ensuring that you are able to support a wide range of events.

This handbook is primarily aimed at people taking the NVQ Level 2 in Spectator Safety, but also provides complete coverage of the learning outcomes for the Award in Understanding Stewarding at Spectator Events.

Bridging the Gap

The *Bridging the Gap* project is a collaboration between education, the private security industry and various agencies involved in the organisation of London 2012 Olympic and Paralympic Games. It aims to provide a 6,000–8,000 strong workforce for employment as security staff at the events and venues involved in the 2012 Olympic Games. It will achieve this by training groups of students, drawn largely from further education colleges on public services courses, as well as individuals from security companies, higher education and the unemployed.

These individuals will work with security companies on a range of events leading up to London 2012, with supervision from tutors who will manage their student/employee teams at Games time. This will transform the relationship between the security industry, uniformed services and the further education sector. After 2012, as part of the legacy of the Games, these experienced tutors working in over 65 colleges throughout the UK will be in place to teach and deliver courses for thousands of students in partnership with the security industry and uniformed services.

Structure of the NVQ Level 2 Certificate

The Certificate is made up of six mandatory units which sit within the QCF (Qualifications and Credit Framework). Although these units are not exactly the same as the National Occupational standards that make up NVQs, the areas they cover are similar. The table below gives the name of the unit and the unit codes used by the different awarding organisations.

Unit name	Accreditation code	SkillsActive unit code	City and Guilds unit code	Edexcel unit code	*Bridging the Gap* unit code
Prepare for spectator events	Y/501/5137	C29	203	3	1
Control the entry, exit and movement of people at spectator events	H/501/5139	C210	205	5	2
Monitor spectators and deal with crowd problems	Y/501/5140	C211	206	6	3
Help to manage conflict	J/501/5134	C237	201	1	4
Contribute to the work of the team	R/501/5136	A52	202	2	5
Deal with accidents and emergencies	D/501/5138	C35	204	4	6

Unit credits

When you complete a unit successfully you will gain a certain number of credits. The credit value of each unit is shown in the table below.

Unit name	Credit value
Prepare for spectator events	3
Control the entry, exit and movement of people at spectator events	4
Monitor spectators and deal with crowd problems	4
Help to manage conflict	4
Contribute to the work of the team	3
Deal with accidents and emergencies	2

In order to complete the full Level 2 Certificate, you will need to take all six mandatory units in order to gain 20 credits.

The credit value of the unit indicates the size of the unit and approximately how long it will take to achieve. Credit is based on how long an average learner would take to complete a unit, and one credit is roughly equal to ten hours of learning, including time spent in classes or group sessions, tutorials, practical work and assessments.

It also includes any time you spend that is not supervised, for example doing homework, independent research or work experience.

Unit structure

Each unit has several learning outcomes and each of these is broken down into a number of assessment criteria. All the learning outcomes of the unit have to be assessed in order for you to complete the unit. The following example is taken from Unit 203 Prepare for spectator events:

Learning outcome	Assessment criteria
1. Prepare for stewarding activities	1. Follow the registration procedures correctly and on time.
	2. Collect their passes, identification and other resources, looking after these and returning them after the event.
	3. Attend the pre-event briefings as required.
	4. Note all the necessary information which is given at the briefings
	5. Correctly follow the pre-event routines.

Units include the following:

- information about what you need to know and understand ('knowledge and understanding' units)
- knowledge, understanding and practical skills which normally have an element of assessment in the workplace ('competence' units).

How you will be assessed

You can be assessed by a range of different methods, based on the learning outcomes and assessment criteria in the unit. Your assessor or tutor will provide you with help and support throughout the assessment process. Some common assessment methods are described below but others may be used as well:

- knowledge, understanding and skills that you demonstrate through your practice in a work setting and that are observed directly by your assessor

- evidence from an expert witness who may be an experienced practitioner who has worked alongside you, or others with suitable backgrounds who can vouch for your practice

- questions (oral and written) and professional discussion, usually with your assessor, which allows you to talk about what you know

- assignments and projects of different types

- assessment of your work products such as risk assessment, notebook, etc.

- tests

- recognised prior learning.

Sometimes your awarding organisation will insist on a specific method such as a test or an assignment. Again, your tutor or assessor will provide you with help and support to decide the best approach.

How to use this book

This book contains all six mandatory units you need to complete for your Level 2 Certificate.

Each chapter is closely matched to the specification for each unit and follows the unit learning outcomes and assessment criteria — making it easy for you to work through the criteria and be sure you are covering everything you need to know.

Key features of the book

Introduction includes a short overview of the unit so you know what to expect, and lists the learning outcomes from the specification.

Unit 203

Prepare for spectator events

Preparing for spectator events is an essential part of a steward's job. In this unit you will understand your important role in ensuring the safety of all spectators, as well any other people, at a venue. You will look at the prevention and reduction of incidents and accidents and the contribution that stewards make to the provision of safety and customer service at event venues, including crowd control, dealing with complaints, directing customers and working with emergency services to deal promptly with any emergencies.

You will learn how to:
- prepare for stewarding activities
- identify and deal with physical hazards
- search the venue for suspect items.

Best practice checklist – a checklist of key points to remember for different tasks or aspects of your role.

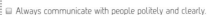

Best Practice Checklist ✔

Helping people with problems

- Always communicate with people politely and clearly.
- Listen attentively and actively at all times.
- Be professional: first impressions are very important.
- Ask if you can help and remain visible and approachable.
- Be aware of a person's particular needs.
- Ensure that you are always impartial.
- Never argue with anyone and get help from a supervisor if you are getting into difficulties.
- Always try and get as much information as possible: find out exactly what the problem is and check your understanding.
- Communicate with the person regularly and let them know what you are doing to help them with the problem.

Case study — real-life scenario exploring key issues to broaden your understanding of key topics; demonstrates how theory relates to everyday practice and poses reflective questions.

Case study

I was posted at the gate of an exhibition which was to run for three days. On the second day, a man showed me a ticket which allowed entry for the first day only. He told me he had been not able to go on that day, and asked if he could be allowed entry for today, as an alternative.

I explained to him that if I allowed him entry there might be a safety problem as the organisers would not know who was in the exhibition hall if there was an emergency. I offered to take him to the box office to see if they would exchange his ticket.

Over to you

☐ How would you have dealt with this customer?

☐ What might have happened if you told the customer there was nothing you could do because he had the wrong ticket, and refused him entry?

Think about it — questions to make you reflect on your experience of work to help you develop and improve.

Think about it

What type of image do you portray?

How can you improve your behaviour and appearance and make sure that it is the right level?

Skills builder — short activities linked to the unit that are designed to develop your professional skills.

Skills builder

It can be difficult at first to listen to someone speaking and at the same time write down important information. You should practise doing this regularly, even using a news programme on the radio or TV. Don't try to write everything down, just some key words that will help you remember the important points.

Key terms — throughout the book technical words and phrases are picked out in bold to make them easy to spot. A simple definition of each key term appears in the margin. All the key terms and their definitions are collected in the glossary at the back of the book.

Key term

Licensable activity: a licensable activity is determined by the role that is performed and the activity undertaken. These are described fully in Section 3 and Schedule 2 of the Private Security Industry Act 2001 (as amended).

At the end of each unit you will find the following pages.

Working Life page that contains:

- **My story** – a case study from an event steward, that focuses on a key aspect from the unit

- **Ask the expert** – questions and answers relating to working practice

- **Top tips** – quick tips to bear in mind to help you if you find yourself in a similar situation.

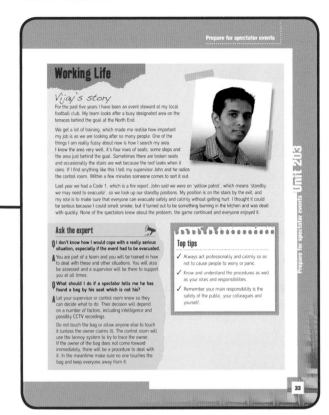

Check your knowledge – a set of questions that will help you consolidate your understanding of the unit's content and ensure you are ready to move on to the next unit.

Getting ready for assessment – summarises what you be assessed on for each unit, and the methods likely to be used.

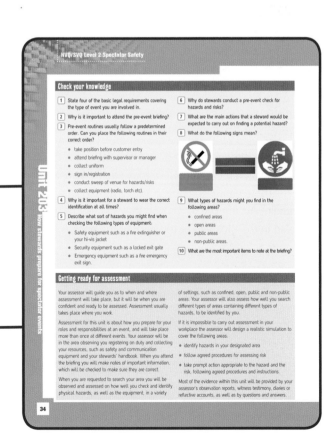

Summary of evidence requirements and assessment methods

Unit	Evidence of real work activity must be supplied for the following, as a minimum	Simulation allowed?	Supplementary evidence can only be used for items that do not require evidence of real work activity. Additional info for each unit is included below.
Support the work of the team and organisation	• Two types of colleagues • Both types of communication	Only for the type of colleague responsible to you and only if there is no naturally occurring evidence	Questioning is allowed for 3.8 if no naturally occurring evidence is available.
Prepare for spectator events	• Three types of resources • All types of information • Three types of equipment • Three types of hazards • All types of areas	For 2.3, 2.4 and 2.5 only, if there is no naturally occurring evidence is available.	n/a
Control the entry, exit and movement of people at spectator events	• Three types of resources • All types of information • Three types of equipment • Three types of hazards • All types of areas	Allowed for the whole of learning outcome 1 and 2 only if there is no naturally occurring evidence is available.	Questioning is allowed for 2.4 if no naturally occurring evidence is available.
Monitor spectators and deal with crowd problems	• Two types of resources • Two types of crowds • All types of areas • Four types of crowd problems (LO1) / three types of crowd problems (LO2) • Two types of people	Not allowed for this unit.	n/a
Help to manage conflict	• All types of methods • Two types of people • All types of procedures	For the whole of learning outcomes 1 and 2 only if there is no naturally occurring evidence is available.	Questioning is allowed for 2.2 if no naturally occurring evidence is available.
Deal with accidents and emergencies	• One type of casualty • One type of qualified assistance • One type of condition • One type of property • Two types of equipment and materials.	Allowed for this unit only if there is no naturally occurring evidence.	Supplementary evidence is allowed for 2.5 only, if there is no naturally occurring evidence is available.

Adapted from QCF Evidence Requirements and Assessment Guidance, Level 2 NVQ Certificate in Spectator Safety with kind permission from SkillsActive. The full document is available from the SkillsActive website.

Unit 203

Prepare for spectator events

Preparing for spectator events is an essential part of a steward's job. In this unit you will understand your important role in ensuring the safety of all spectators, as well any other people, at a venue. You will look at the prevention and reduction of incidents and accidents and the contribution that stewards make to the provision of safety and customer service at event venues, including crowd control, dealing with complaints, directing customers and working with emergency services to deal promptly with any emergencies.

You will learn how to:
☐ prepare for stewarding activities
☐ identify and deal with physical hazards
☐ search the venue for suspect items.

Prepare for stewarding activities
Maintain standards of behaviour and appearance

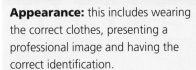

Key terms

Appearance: this includes wearing the correct clothes, presenting a professional image and having the correct identification.

Venue: the grounds or building where an event takes place.

Standards of **appearance** are important, as people look for someone in authority who looks professional when they require assistance. Would you feel comfortable approaching someone for help if they looked untidy, scruffy and dirty? Or would you rather go to someone who looked smart and professional? Image and first impressions are very important and you should be aware of your appearance at all times.

Do you always check your appearance before you start work?

Think about it

What type of image do you portray?

How can you improve your behaviour and appearance and make sure that it is the right level?

Standards of behaviour are also very important. Members of the public need to feel safe and secure in your presence, so you will also find that your company, as well as the venue you are working at, will insist on standards of behaviour and appearance. You are also playing a major role in customer relations at the **venue**; your attitude goes a very long way to making sure that the customers enjoy the event.

Table 203.1 outlines some aspects of behaviour and the reasons certain standards should be maintained. Can you think of any behaviour that would not be permitted under the headings given in the table and why this would be?

Steward's behaviour	Reasons (examples)
Manner and general conduct	<ul><li>professional standards</li><li>image</li><li>safety</li><li>customer care</li></ul>
Smoking, eating and drinking on duty	<ul><li>smoking is against the law in public buildings</li><li>poor first impression (reflecting on you, your company and the venue)</li><li>unprofessional</li></ul>
Currently taking prescription medication	May not be able to deal with certain incidents (always let supervisor know)
Alcohol, drugs and gambling	High risk (see all previous reasons)

Table 203.1 Maintaining standards of behaviour and appearance

A number of basic values underpin good practice, and these values are written into the Code of Conduct for Spectator Safety in the *Guide to Safety at Sports Grounds* 5th edition (see Figure 203.1).

CODE OF CONDUCT

- Stewards should at all times be polite, courteous and helpful to all spectators, regardless of their affiliations.

- Stewards should be smartly dressed at all times. Their appearance should be clean and tidy.

- Stewards are not employed, hired or contracted to watch the event. They should concentrate on their duties and responsibilities at all times.

- Stewards should never:
  - o wear clothing that may appear partisan or may cause offence while on duty
  - o celebrate or show extreme reaction to the event
  - o eat, drink or smoke in view of the public
  - o consume alcohol before or during the event
  - o use obscene, offensive or intimidatory language or gestures.

Figure 203.1 Example of a code of conduct

Functional skills

English: Reading the code of conduct and converting it into a good practice checklist before attending an event will help you improve your functional skills in English.

Roles and responsibilities of an event steward

The role that an event steward plays in the preparation of an event is crucial to the overall spectator experience and ultimately the event's success. The importance of an event steward cannot be overstated, and you will be expected to have a number of personal skills and attributes (see Figure 203.2).

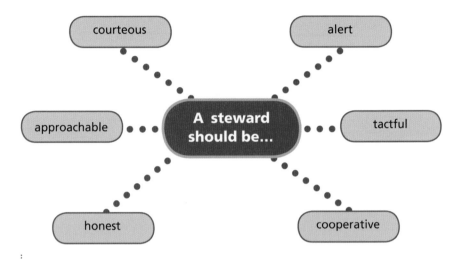

courteous

alert

approachable

A steward should be...

tactful

honest

cooperative

Figure 203.2 The personal skills and attributes of a steward

Roles

Event stewards can be asked to perform a number of different roles either as individuals or as part of a team, including any of the following:

☐ crowd control

☐ dealing with complaints

☐ customer-care duties such as directing customers to seats, refreshment areas, toilets and first aid facilities

☐ ensuring the safety of the public by providing advice and assistance

☐ providing guidance and direction to visitors arriving by car or on foot, including the management of internal roadway crossings to ensure safe passage

☐ being responsible for the health, safety and comfort of spectators within a designated area

☐ reporting to a supervisor any damage or defects likely to pose a risk to spectators' health and safety, such as damaged seats or barriers

☐ working alongside **emergency services**, e.g. providing assistance in carrying out evacuation procedures

☐ providing assistance to people requiring help

Key term

Emergency services: usually the fire service, ambulance service or police.

- monitoring and maintaining the pedestrian flow at key locations such as entry and exit points
- watching for any risk or hazard, e.g. ensuring gangways and exit/evacuation routes are kept clear for health and safety purposes
- checking invitations, wristbands or tickets on entry or exit.

Responsibilities

Event stewards are expected to:

- report on time
- be clean and presentable with full uniform
- pay full attention during pre-event briefing
- ensure that a venue sweep (search) is comprehensive and leaves no missed areas
- assist any customer as best they can
- proactively deal with or report illegal or unsociable behaviour
- report crowd control problems immediately.

Further responsibilities include:

- responding to emergencies (such as the early stages of a fire)
- carrying out pre-event safety checks
- providing the public with information about layout, facilities etc.
- staffing entrances, exits and other strategic points (health and safety)
- recognising and responding to crowd conditions to ensure safe movement, dispersal and prevention of overcrowding
- investigating disturbances or incidents (not dealing with them)
- communicating with the control centre.

The lists relating to roles and responsibilities, as well as to duties and competencies, might seem enormous, but most are common sense and will be well covered in your training.

Legal limitations of the role of an event steward

There are also legal limits covering the role of stewards at **spectator events**. For example, unless an event steward holds a Security Industry Authority licence and is there to provide a visible security presence they cannot legally:

- restrict access to a VIP area

- respond to incidents within crowds, queues or the audience to control behaviour which is antisocial, undesirable or likely to be of harm to others

- perform door supervisor duties in a licensed area

- screen a person's suitability to enter the venue, for example, people under the influence of alcohol or drugs or demonstrating antisocial behaviour

- search people and/or property entering an event to prevent unauthorised or illegal items from entering the premises, e.g. cameras, alcohol, drugs or weapons

- eject individuals from a venue, event or designated area, including the pit or backstage areas

- carry out any duties defined as 'security duties', such as protecting the pitch, track or other area from spectators or others to prevent damage to property or people

- prevent and detect crime within a designated area (though they may respond as an individual citizen to prevent a crime occurring if in a position to do so)

- guard a property and/or equipment during the set up and breakdown of an event or exhibition

- patrol the perimeter of an event to prevent unauthorised access, for example, by individuals climbing or breaching fences or barriers

- patrol the venue, observe from a fixed position or monitor CCTV footage.

Key term

Spectator event: this could be any type of public event or performance, including sporting.

Are you aware of the type of activities that are licensed and that you should therefore not perform as an event steward?

 Remember: The roles and responsibilities of an event steward are different from those of a person who holds an SIA licence. The work you do will determine whether or not you need a licence.

There are a minimum number of stewards required to run an event and this depends on a number of factors, including the size and type of crowd, the type of venue and risk assessment. Not having enough stewards can have major implications for crowd safety and would breach the Safety Certificate. Event stewards are also required to be trained.

Responsibilities at different types of events

An event steward could be involved in many different types of event, including:

- sporting events (e.g. football, rugby, cricket, car racing, horse racing)
- musical events (e.g. concerts, festivals, raves)
- agricultural shows, motor shows, air shows
- parades, village fêtes, continental markets
- under-18 discos
- exhibitions
- conferences
- marathons or fun runs
- surfing festivals
- maritime events.

What type of events are held in your area?

Key terms

Policies: what an organisation says its staff should and should not do in certain situations.

Procedures: a way of carrying out policies as part of an activity or process.

Each event may also have its own **policies**, **procedures** and individual circumstances which can affect an event steward's role. For example:

- A music festival pit compared with a local authority event pit. At a local authority event the role of the steward may be to prevent illegal access to the stage rather than deal with crowd issues, which are not usually expected.

- Family-orientated events compared with rock music festivals. The role here is based on pre-event risk assessment of anticipated crowd behaviour carried out by the event safety officer. For example, umbrellas may be allowed into a family-orientated event but not at a rock music festival where they are more likely to be used as offensive weapons.

- A dance music concert and an agricultural show. A dance music concert may require SIA-licensed staff to search for drugs in addition to stewards checking for tickets; at an agricultural show the role is more likely to be confined to checking tickets.

What sort of duties would you expect to perform at this type of event?

Show awareness of relevant safety guidance documents at events

Most of the information and guidance on safety at events can be found within the following documents:

- the *Guide to Safety at Sports Grounds*, 5th edition. For a link to this document please go to www.pearsonhotlinks.co.uk, search for this title and click on the relevant page.

- venue- and event-specific documentation relating to safety management, graduated response and contingency plans

- the stewards' handbook

- ground regulations for football and rugby.

The following guidance documents are used by all people involved in the event industry.

Title of document	What it covers	When you need it
Guide to Safety at Sports Grounds – also known as 'The Green Guide' (FLA)	This is a document produced by the Football Licensing Authority outlining guidance for the safe running of sporting grounds and their events. It does not form a legal requirement but offers guidance on legal requirements. The document can be accessed online or bought from The Stationery Office.	This is a useful document used regularly by safety officers, event managers, relevant authorities and stewarding companies.
Managing Crowd Safety in Public Venues (HSE)	This is a Health and Safety Executive document that provides guidance for the owners and managers of venues and enforcement authorities, on crowd behaviour and the effects of crowds on safety.	A useful guidance document consulted by safety officers, event managers, relevant authorities and stewarding companies.
The event safety guide 'The Purple Guide'	This is a Health and Safety Executive-produced document outlining guidance for health, safety and welfare at music and similar events. It can be accessed online or bought from The Stationery Office.	For use by event organisers, applicable to enforcement officers, emergency services and other contractors.
The Northern Ireland Guide to Safety at Sports Grounds 'The Red Guide'	This is a document produced by the Northern Ireland Department of Culture, Arts and Leisure, and Sports Northern Ireland. It is the Northern Ireland version of 'The Green Guide' with Northern Ireland specifics, such as stadium design and law. Available to buy from The Stationery Office.	Used regularly by safety officers, event managers, relevant authorities and stewarding companies.
SIA Guidance Document 'Security at Events'	Produced by the Security Industry Authority, this guide offers guidance on when SIA licences are required at events. Available to download from the SIA website.	For use by event organisers, venue managers, safety officers, event stewarding companies, security guarding and door supervisor companies.
Specific policies and procedures of employer, event or venue	• Health and safety policy • Risk assessment procedure • Event safety management plan All venues must have a health and safety policy, as well as a procedure for carrying out risk assessment and an event safety management plan.	For event organisers, venue managers, safety officers, event stewarding companies, emergency services.

Table 203.2 Examples of guidance documents

Basic legal requirements for different types of events

There are numerous Acts of Parliament covering events and the licences and documents they require. These include:

☐ the Health and Safety at Work Act 1974

☐ the Safety of Sports Grounds Act 1975

☐ the Fire Safety and Places of Sports Act 1987

☐ the Sporting Events (Control of Alcohol etc.) Act 1985

Table 203.3 shows some examples of the legal requirements for various types of event.

Key term 🔑

Licensable activity: a licensable activity is determined by the role that is performed and the activity undertaken. These are described fully in Section 3 and Schedule 2 of the Private Security Industry Act 2001 (as amended).

Legal requirement	Reason
Entertainment licence	Most public entertainment events need a licence whether or not there is an admission charge, to ensure that an event is safe and comfortable for visitors. The local authority will inspect facilities to assess: ● disabled access and facilities ● sanitation ● noise pollution ● firefighting equipment ● the likelihood of overcrowding. Without a licence the event would be illegal.
Premises licence	Authorises the sale of alcohol, supply of alcohol to a club member, provision of entertainment, provision of late-night refreshment (hot food or drink between the hours of 23:00 and 05:00).
Temporary events notice	Required if an event intends to carry out **licensable activity** on unlicensed premises, and covers the sale and supply of alcohol, music, singing and dancing, or late-night refreshment. There are special conditions covering the number of times the licence can be used in a calendar year and the maximum number of people allowed at an event (499 at any one time). (Licensing Act 2003)
Insurance cover	Normally: ● public liability insurance (the amount of cover depends on the risk) ● product liability insurance ● employers' liability insurance
Risk assessment	A requirement for all events. See the Health and Safety Executive's guide, *Five steps to risk assessment*. (INDG163 REV2).
Food hygiene	Food hygiene legislation applies to any activity that involves handling food (including drinks, e.g. tea, coffee, beer).

Table 203.3 Examples of legal requirements

Table 203.3 Examples of legal requirements (cont.)

Legal requirement	Reason
Health and Safety at Work Act 1974	All events need to comply with legislation regarding health and safety. It is also the organiser's responsibility to notify police, fire and rescue services and the ambulance service, the county council and the Maritime and Coastguard Agency if the activity is water based. These authorities may not need to be involved but should always be informed. Larger, high-risk events may require a local authority Safety Advisory Group. *The event safety guide: A guide to health, safety and welfare at music and similar events* (The Purple Guide), produced by the Health and Safety Executive, contains information needed by event organisers, their contractors and employees to fulfil the requirements of the 1974 Act and associated regulations. Further information can be found on the Health and Safety Executive entertainment web pages. For a link to their website please visit www.pearsonhotlinks.co.uk
Noise control (Environmental Protection Act)	Local authorities and environmental health departments deal with complaints concerning noise from events and licensed premises and, where necessary, can take enforcement action under the Licensing Act 2003. Noise control will be an integral part of the planning of an event.
Safety of Sports Grounds Act 1975	All sports stadia with a spectator capacity of more than 10,000 people are designated by the government and must be certified under the Safety of Sports Grounds Act. A special safety certificate will need to be granted by the local authority setting out the following minimum standards for: • structural integrity of the stand/stadia • provisions for means of escape • adequate fire precautions • emergency services coordination • provision of suitable management strategies (i.e., stewarding, crowd control, match-day safety arrangements, evacuation procedures, contingency plans etc.).
Fire Safety and Places of Sports Act 1987	This provides for a system of safety certification by local authorities for 'regulated stands' at sports grounds. Applies to all outdoor sports grounds that accommodate at least 500 spectators (seated or standing).
Sporting Events (Control of Alcohol etc.) Act 1985	This Act sets out the provisions to deal with and prevent: • consumption of alcohol within view of the playing area (not within the ground) • a drunk person entering a football ground while a designated football match is taking place • consumption of alcohol on certain coaches, trains and motor vehicles travelling to a designated football match • possession of fireworks, flares or similar.
Street Collection Permit	Many events will also involve street collections for charities and will need to obtain a licence for the event and for those collecting money from the council. Examples of this include 'moving collections' at carnivals.
Road Closure Order and Temporary Orders	Local councils have the power under the Town Police Clauses Act 1847 to close roads for public events such as carnivals.
Street Trading Licence	On the approach to many events people may be selling goods, such as programmes, memorabilia, fanzines (magazines), photographs, clothes etc., and will require a licence to trade.

There are many more laws, guidelines and regulations that determine organisations' policies and procedures, depending on the type of event involved. Event stewards are not expected to know the details of this legislation, but it is useful to know they exist and how they can affect your role.

Collect your passes, identification and other resources, looking after these and returning them after the event

When you register you will be provided with a number of important resources such as a pass for the area where you are working and an identification badge. It is important that everyone attending an event can easily recognise you as a steward, in case they need help in an incident or an answer to a problem. Apart from police officers you are likely to be the people who are most easily identified. You will also need to be identifiable by your **colleagues** and the emergency services in the event of an **emergency**, so the incident can be managed and controlled.

You also need to wear identification so that event managers know you are a trained steward who is authorised to be at that event. Although this might seem obvious, at a large event your managers may not know all the stewards, and people sometimes wear high-visibility clothing into an event in order to pass as an official steward. Identification will therefore contain your name, company, date and event as proof that you are authorised to act as a steward. You might also wear a wrist band authorising entry to a specific area.

Key terms 🔑

Colleagues: the people you work with (those working at your own level and your managers).

Emergency: any situation that immediately threatens the health and safety of spectators, staff or yourself, for example, fires or bomb threats.

Figure 203.3 Example of an ID card

Your identification is very important – you must take care of these resources and hand them back at the end of the event.

Other important resources or information you could be provided with include:

☐ **communications** equipment, such as:

- radio, with earpiece and microphone
- location of telephones
- location of megaphones

Key term 🔑

Communications resources: these could be notebooks for recording incidents, or communications equipment such as radios, if appropriate.

☐ safety equipment, such as:

- high-visibility vests/jackets
- waterproofs
- sun cream
- hats
- gloves
- water
- torches
- earplugs
- first aid kit.

Think about it

Why might your supervisor provide you with a torch at a sports event in a stadium taking place in the middle of a sunny afternoon?

What are you going to do if you check your torch an hour after the event has started and discover it doesn't work?

Procedures for checking resources and reporting faults

You must check all resources and equipment to ensure they are working correctly – these resources could be very important during an incident and will be used at the next event. Any failure of equipment such as radios and torches must be reported immediately: test all equipment when it is issued to you and half way through the event. This will show up any faults and whether or not it is still available for use. Don't forget to hand back the equipment at the end of the event, and report any faults or failures.

You will also receive a stewards' (or safety) handbook, as well as:

☐ a map of key points

☐ a timetable of events.

The handbook is an important document and may contain the following information:

☐ venue regulations

☐ emergency and evacuation procedures

☐ layout of venue (plan)

☐ health and safety information

☐ who's who (management structure)

☐ stewards' duties

☐ customer care.

Skills builder

How would you check the following items were in good working order and fit for purpose? What would you do if you found a fault?

- torch
- ear plugs
- first aid kit
- passes/identification
- radio
- high-visibility clothing

Remember: Read and understand the stewards' handbook. This relates to security and safety and may contain evacuation procedures, venue regulations, layout and a map of the venue, as well as other information concerning the comfort and safety of staff and visitors, such as where to obtain first aid, refreshments, disabled and other facilities, emergency exits and firefighting equipment.

C
E
C

Colminster Exhibition Centre

Stewards' Handbook

Trade Conference

5 – 7 April 2011

Figure 203.4 Example of a stewards' handbook

Skills builder

It can be difficult at first to listen to someone speaking and at the same time write down important information. You should practise doing this regularly, even using a news programme on the radio or TV. Don't try to write everything down, just some key words that will help you remember the important points.

Attend registration and pre-event briefings as required

Registration will involve reporting to a supervisor at a pre-determined location in a clean and presentable uniform which identifies you as a steward, and attending a pre-event briefing. It is vital that you attend registration correctly and on time. Collect your pass, identification and other resources and note all the necessary information given at the briefings. Registration also allows the safety officer, the local authority or the management at the venue to count the number of stewards attending. This is a health and safety requirement, as there can be serious implications if not enough stewards are present to provide for the safety of people attending an event.

When you report to work you should notify your supervisor (or the person registering you) if you have any medical issues that could affect your role as a steward, or any religious requirements that will affect your duties, for example, prayer time, or restrictions involving working at specific venues or events.

If you come to work under the influence of alcohol (even from the night before) you will be sent off site and possibly disciplined. Don't use any non-prescribed drugs while working, and if you are using prescribed medication that may affect your work then inform your supervisor. Your supervisor must know if something is affecting you, as your role as steward is to look after a section of the crowd, sometimes in emergency conditions.

 Remember: It is important that you register on time, collect your uniform and resources and attend the briefing.

Think about it

In what order would you do the following activities?

- Attend the pre-event briefings as required and note all necessary information given at these briefings.
- Look after your pass, identification and other resources and return them after the event.
- Collect your pass, identification and other resources.
- Correctly follow all pre-event routines.

At the briefing, you and other members of your team, including supervisors, the police and first aid personnel, will be provided with details about the event, customer care, safety, **risks** and communication methods.

You will also be provided with a written statement of your duties, a plan showing key features, instructions on how you are expected to **communicate** and what to do in the event of a major incident.

Key terms

Risk: the likelihood of a hazard causing harm and the seriousness of this harm.

Communicate: by using words, as well as body language, tone of voice, etc.

The briefing will be a formal session and follow a set agenda — usually following what is known as the IIMARCH briefing standard. IIMARCH stands for Information, Intention, Method, Administration, Risk assessment, Communication, Human rights.

Information: the details of the event and any anticipated problems, for example, the type of event and any information you need to know. This will normally include:

- number of people attending
- anticipated weather conditions
- travelling arrangements of the public
- information relating to any VIPs attending
- the provision of first aid
- police intelligence
- club/event intelligence
- previous history of similar events
- particular problems in or around the event
- plans for crowd segregation
- police presence.

Intention: the customer care, wellbeing and safety-management strategies and objectives, for example:

- the arrangements made for the health and safety of the crowd
- their care and comfort
- what is expected of stewards, staff etc.
- how the venue rules will be enforced.

Method: the tactics for achieving these strategies and objectives, for example:

- safety checks (those already carried out as well as those you will need to do)
- points of entry into the venue, including restricted access
- evacuation procedures and code words
- control structure (the chain of command — who is responsible)
- supervision (who your supervisor will be)
- deployment (where you will be sent — what your duties are)
- ticketing (types of ticketing arrangements for this event)

☐ **debriefing** arrangements (where you will be debriefed and what time this will occur).

Administration: general issues, including your role at the event and any refreshment breaks, as well as any forms used to record incidents. Examples include:

☐ the location of forms such as RIDDOR (Reporting of Injuries, Diseases and Dangerous Occurrences) and accident forms

☐ incident report sheets

☐ catering arrangements and refreshment breaks

☐ return of equipment.

Risk assessment: the main risks for the event and the contingencies for dealing with them. Before any event occurs a detailed risk assessment will be carried out by the safety officer, usually in conjunction with partners such as the emergency services, local authority and the event management company. The risk assessment will focus on a number of key areas such as those in Table 203.4.

Key term

Debrief: feeding back information relating to the way the event was managed and any incidents that occurred.

Hazards	Vehicle movements
What could go wrong?	Collision with pedestrians
Who may be harmed?	Staff, public, contractors
What is currently in place to help control the risk?	• Vehicles and pedestrian access/egress separated • Event starts at 14:00: vehicle movements should occur between 10:00 and 13:00 • Event closes at 19:00: vehicle movements should occur between 15:30 and 16:30 • During periods of vehicle movement, vehicles are only permitted to travel in one direction at set times.
Is the risk currently high, medium or low?	Medium
What extra controls need to be in place?	• Vehicle marshalling to be introduced • Marshals to wear high-visibility vests/jackets • After event, site to be cleared of pedestrians before vehicles are admitted • Only marshals in high-visibility clothing are to be in the area during vehicle movements.
By when?	Saturday 10th August
By whom?	Safety officer

Table 203.4 Example of a typical risk assessment

Prepare for spectator events **Unit 203**

Key terms

Hazard: anything with the potential to cause harm (e.g. electricity, hazardous substances, excessive noise).

Hygiene hazard: anything causing a risk to hygiene, for example, unsanitary toilets.

Other **hazards** depend on the venue but might include:

- ☐ lack of access for emergency services
- ☐ insufficient and/or unsuitable first aid cover
- ☐ poor supervision of event
- ☐ poor supervision of children
- ☐ **hygiene hazards**
- ☐ welfare facilities
- ☐ disposal of waste.

Communication: the means by which personnel will be informed and directed; also the receiving of feedback to identify any ongoing issues. For example:

- ☐ details of stewards and supervisors who will be issued with radios
- ☐ the radio channels to be used
- ☐ number of radios
- ☐ control room facilities
- ☐ mobile telephones being used and numbers
- ☐ details of an incident control room and call signs
- ☐ responsibilities of personnel manning the control room and incident control.

Human rights: all briefings must contain written considerations on human rights issues. These will pay attention to the following questions:

- ☐ Are human rights being taken into consideration when making the plans for the event – are the plans proportional?
- ☐ Is what the management of the event is trying to achieve permitted by law?
- ☐ Are areas of the venue accessible to members of the public with mobility issues?
- ☐ Is the information contained within the briefing and the risk assessment accessible to the public if requested and authorised?
- ☐ Does what the management is planning to do have a legitimate aim?

Take notes during the briefing so you can refer to them later

Note all the necessary information given at the briefings

You will be provided with a lot of information during the briefing; this can be categorised as 'need to know' and 'nice to know' information. First of all, you must know what time to register and attend the briefing!

Need to know (vital information for you to carry out your role)

For example:

☐ your exact role at the event

☐ evacuation procedures

- running times of show/event
- attendance figures and audience profile
- event profile
- type and location of first aid
- ground regulations (if applicable)
- emergency telephone locations
- stewarding procedures
- potential hazards and risks

Nice to know (information to improve customer care)

For example:

- location of bars, toilets, cash machines, food outlets etc.
- transport information — parking facilities, taxis/buses/trains
- merchandise stands
- programme sellers
- box office
- location of the lost property office and lost children point.

During the briefing you will also be informed about the chain of command and the responsibilities of individuals and teams, emergency code words and procedures and radio call signs. This is a typical event 'chain of command'.

Skills builder

When you attend your next pre-event briefing, listen carefully to all the information and write notes so you can refer to them later. Ask questions if there is anything you are not sure about.

Ask your supervisor to go through procedures with you, such as:

- how you should communicate with your supervisor if you are not supplied with a radio
- where the nearest first aid point is for your designated area
- anything in particular you need to be aware of in your designated area.

When you get to your area, try to locate all the different facilities before the public arrives.

Functional skills

English: Writing — when taking notes during a pre-event briefing, you will be using your English writing skills.

Correctly follow pre-event routines

Pre-event routines are carried out as part of the preparation for an event and before the public are admitted. Full checks are carried out within **designated areas**, to make sure everything is as safe as possible and any potential hazards are dealt with.

You will cover searching your designated area as part of a pre-event routine in more detail on page 30.

more detail on page 30.

Key term

Designated area: the area you are responsible for.

Arrive at venue and sign in

Sign out uniform

Check and sign out equipment

Attend briefing

Check your area for hazards

Take position before start

Figure 203.5 Example of a pre-event routine

Identify and deal with physical hazards

Follow agreed procedures to check equipment

Every venue will have a procedure you will need to follow when checking equipment, which you will normally carry out under supervision before the event opens to the public. The types of equipment involved will depend on where you have been deployed to. Examples of equipment could be:

- safety barriers
- fire equipment
- phones
- **tannoy system**
- radios
- loud hailers.

This is all part of the risk assessment to make sure that potential hazards have been identified and dealt with. If the equipment is faulty, you will have time to report it so someone can put it right.

Key term

Tannoy system: a public address system usually in the form of a series of loudspeakers positioned around the ground so that important messages can be relayed to visitors and staff at an event.

Safety barriers help to control crowds

Know the meaning of relevant safety signs and notices

Most of the safety equipment you will need to check will have a sign near to it; you will be expected to know what the signs mean.

Here are some examples of safety signs that you are likely to see. Mandatory means that you must carry out the instruction. They are coloured blue. Warning signs are red or yellow. Signs giving information are green.

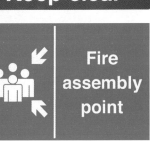

Examples of some safety signs

Key term

Assess: gather all necessary information relating to a crowd problem and work out the level of risk to yourself and others.

Think about it

You have been asked to check the safety barriers in your area before the start of a very busy event, and you notice that three of the barriers have damaged feet and hooks, weakening the barricade strength.

Write down three of the most important things you should do to reduce the risk.

How would you:

- **assess** the seriousness of the hazard
- report the hazard
- deal with the hazard?

Identify hazards in their designated area

Before the public arrives, you will be asked to carry out a sweep, or search, of your designated area. This initial sweep is for physical hazards, so you will need to check that:

☐ there are no damaged barriers, chairs or other equipment

☐ there are no accessible items that could be used as missiles

☐ there is no accumulation of combustible waste or hazardous materials

☐ all entry and exit routes are free from obstruction.

All hazards have the potential to cause disruption if they are not dealt with effectively. Examples could be a wet floor caused by a water leak, which has to be taped off to prevent the public from slipping; broken chairs will mean extra seating will have to be found for ticket holders; damaged safety barriers which, if not repaired quickly or replaced, could contribute to major disruption during an event.

Check your understanding

Why do we conduct venue sweeps before customers arrive?

What are we checking for?

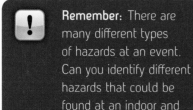

Remember: There are many different types of hazards at an event. Can you identify different hazards that could be found at an indoor and outdoor event?

If you have identified a hazard, make sure it is dealt with, or clearly signed, so it doesn't cause an accident

Follow agreed procedures for assessing risk and take appropriate action

A risk assessment involves deciding how likely it is that damage, loss or injury will be caused by a hazard and how severe the outcome may be. There will be a procedure for assessing the risk of the hazard, which requires you to look at all the surrounding circumstances, including:

☐ the location of the hazard

☐ the time it was found

☐ the likelihood of it leading to an injury

☐ how serious an injury it could cause.

Think about the hazards and risks involved when you enter a venue (Figure 203.6 illustrates this process). For example, there could be a slip hazard on a staircase due to a discarded banana skin! At the other end of the scale there could be a build-up of rubbish under a wooden stadium, increasing the risk of a fire.

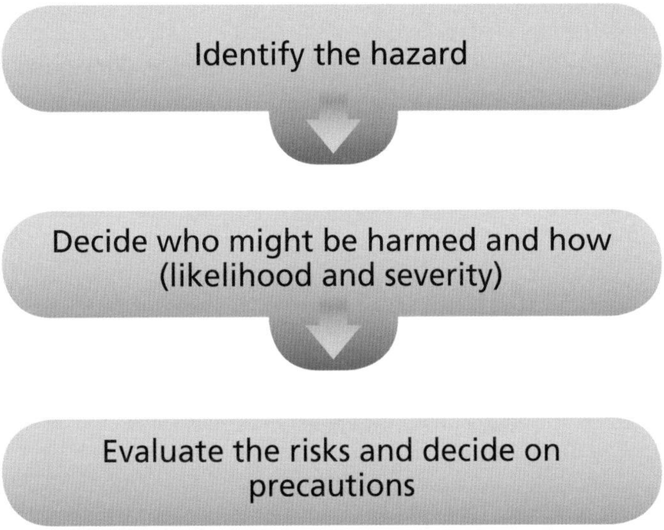

Identify the hazard

Decide who might be harmed and how
(likelihood and severity)

Evaluate the risks and decide on
precautions

Figure 203.6 A simple hazard and risk diagram

The main actions a steward would be expected to carry out on finding a potential hazard would be:

☐ remove the hazard if possible

☐ restrict access to the hazard

☐ report the hazard to your supervisor.

Once you have reported a hazard, you must make sure that no one enters the area. You could stand by the area and direct people away from it, close off the area with barriers or tape, or bring in other stewards to form a barrier.

The Health and Safety at Work Act is very clear about the duty of people at work, including stewards. The law states that:

It is your responsibility to look after yourself and others by taking reasonable care of health and safety by what you do or by what you do not do.

Failing to take action, by ignoring or not dealing with a hazard, or failing to notify others, could result in a major incident and make you liable under the law. Never ignore a hazard under any circumstances.

Case study

It was 2pm on a sunny afternoon in June and I noticed lots of fans arriving at a football match by bus, which stops across the other side of a main road. They were dressed in black (the colour of their team). They got off the bus and crossed over the road to a large busy car park, which they then had to go through to reach the gate of the venue.

Over to you

☐ What are the hazards so far, and what are the risks?

☐ Do the risk factors change if you use the same circumstances above, but change the time and weather conditions? For example, if the fans leave the event at 10:30pm, it is dark and raining, and they are dressed in black.

☐ What level of risk is there to pedestrians in the car park area?

☐ Is there a likelihood of getting injured by a vehicle? How serious might it be?

☐ Suggest three ways of making it safer for pedestrians in the car park area, and therefore reducing the risk.

Functional skills

English: Writing and speaking — carry out a risk assessment, write it down and explain your work to another person on your course.

Following on from the case study earlier, some possible precautions you could have suggested include:

☐ Pedestrians could wear fluorescent jackets and carry torches for the return journey.

☐ Is there any alternative route, rather than through the busy car park? Could pedestrians walk around it?

☐ Barriers could be placed in the car park creating space for pedestrians and separate space used for vehicles.

☐ Stewards in the car park could direct traffic and pedestrian flow.

☐ Police officers could be put in charge of directing traffic and pedestrian movement on the road.

☐ Better lighting could be installed on the car park and road.

Case study

When I attended the training to be a qualified event steward, we were told about the terrible disaster that took place at Valley Parade, Bradford Football Stadium on 11 May 1985, where 56 supporters died and 265 were injured. The death toll might have been higher had it not been for the courage of police officers and 22 spectators who were later presented with bravery awards. The fire is thought to have been caused by the accidental dropping of a match or a cigarette stubbed out in a polystyrene cup, and the resulting fire was fuelled by rubbish underneath the wooden stand.

I learnt how things have changed since then following an inquiry chaired by Sir Oliver Popplewell, which made 32 recommendations for new legislation covering safety at sports grounds across the UK.

At the training I was asked to think about how the fire started and what happened when people were trying to escape.

Over to you

☐ The Popplewell Inquiry changed the way football stands were built, and clubs had to remove old ones and rebuild them. Why do you think they did this?

☐ Why are spectators no longer penned into the stands by high perimeter fences at football grounds?

☐ Why do event stewards receive training which includes so much information and guidance relating to health and safety?

Aftermath of the fire at Valley Parade, Bradford Football Stadium in 1985

Communicate verbally and non-verbally with colleagues and other people involved

Skills builder

There are a number of correct methods of communication. You might not have a radio or access to a phone but you will always be part of a team with a supervisor, so help will never be far away. Always let your colleagues and/or supervisor know about problems as soon as possible. What other methods of communication can be used to pass messages?

You will be required to communicate hazards clearly and quickly to colleagues and others, to make sure that they know about the risks involved and can take action. Never put yourself or others at risk by failing to communicate.

Each event and venue will have its own reporting procedure, which will be clearly communicated during the briefing and in your handbook.

You could communicate with your colleagues using the following methods:

- ☐ a fixed telephone point in your designated area
- ☐ a radio or mobile phone
- ☐ hand signals
- ☐ alert codes (e.g., some events use a 'traffic light' colour system, such as that shown in Figure 203.7).

Alert state	Operational state
RED	Evacuate
YELLOW (AMBER)	Alert is being assessed. Stand by positions to be taken up as action may be required
GREEN	No alert – situation is normal
Type of incident	**Code**
Fire	Code 1
Suspect package	Code 2
Chemical or gas leak	Code 3
Crowd disorder	Code 4
Structural failure	Code 5

NB: these are shown as examples only and will not necessarily be used where you work

Figure 203.7 Example of alert codes table

Make sure that any action is not dangerous for people involved

Earlier in this unit the standards, behaviour and code of conduct for event stewards was highlighted. The Code of Conduct states:

Stewards are not employed, hired or contracted to watch the event. They should at all times concentrate on their duties and responsibilities.

The Health and Safety at Work Act is also very clear about the duty of people at work. Because you are steward you have certain duties under the Act. The law states that:

It is your responsibility to look after yourself and others by taking reasonable care of health and safety by what you do or by what you do not do.

A serious health and safety incident could be caused by any of the following situations:

☐ a hazard was discovered but ignored

☐ you failed to report a hazard

☐ you over-reacted and caused panic by evacuating a large section of the crowd without the full information or without informing your supervisor.

A hazard identified, reported and dealt with promptly removes the risk and becomes a non-event. The main purpose of looking for hazards is to ensure the safety of everyone in the venue, including you.

Search the venue for suspect items

Searches of the event area should be conducted as part of a venue's daily good housekeeping routine, and should also be conducted in response to a specific threat and when there is a heightened response level.

Get information on the type of item being searched for

You may be asked to carry out a specific search of your designated area for **suspect items** (this could involve a search for drink, drugs, or prohibited items such as weapons, flares, or explosive devices). Make sure the information you receive is clear and that you understand exactly what you are being asked to search for. Before you start any search, always be certain about the following:

☐ Why are we searching?

☐ What are we searching for?

☐ How good is the information?

Functional skills

English: Reading – reading pre-event memos, emails or messages – where and when to meet, where to collect resources etc. – map of venue, stewards' handbook will help develop your English reading skills.

English: Writing – taking notes at the pre-event briefing will develop your writing skills.

English: Communication – listening and assimilating information at the briefing, including details of emergency code words and radio call signs, using radios and communicating with the control centre will develop your communication skills.

Key term	

Suspect items: any item which arouses suspicion, such as an unattended bag or package.

▢ What are the risks or hazards?

▢ What do we know?

▢ What do we want to know?

Obtaining this level of information is important for your safety and that of other people. Unless you know exactly what you are looking for, you may well miss the object(s) you are searching for.

Search the designated area thoroughly following instructions

Search plans for each area of a venue will be prepared in advance by the management team, usually the safety officer and security manager. Your designated area could be totally different to another steward's area, and different from the area you are used to working in. In any venue, areas generally fall into the following categories:

▢ confined areas, such as a room, concourse, paddock etc.

▢ open areas, such as a car park, ticket barrier, bowl of a stadium, large field

▢ public areas, where the public have access

▢ private areas, such as back stage or catering areas.

Each area has different needs and will need a different approach to carrying out the search. The overall aim is to make sure that all areas are searched thoroughly and systematically so no part is left unchecked. Your area may also be divided into sectors, so each sector is a manageable size in which to carry out a search. These sectors may be contained in the search plan. The search plan should have a written checklist – signed by your supervisor – for the event security or safety officer.

Remember your search will also include any stairs, fire escapes, corridors, toilets and lifts in the search plan, as well as car parks, service yards and other outside areas. In case of the need for evacuation, a search of assembly areas, their access routes and the surrounding area will also need be made.

You do not need to have expertise in explosives or other suspect items; your main strength is that you know the area so will be able to search properly and quickly, looking for items that are not normally present or cannot be accounted for.

Searching is a team effort, and you will normally search in pairs, making sure that the whole search is conducted carefully and systematically.

Venue opening checks

▢ check all seats are safe

▢ check all cable ramps etc. are clearly marked

▢ check exit signage is correct.

During event checks

- ensure trip hazards are illuminated during darkness

- ensure walkways are kept clear at all times

- ensure spills etc. are reported immediately

- ensure you can see illuminated signage from your position.

> **Remember:** Do not touch or try to move the suspect object. Assess the situation, communicate with your colleagues and/or supervisor and await their decision before action is taken. The procedures will be made clear to you at the briefing and will include your supervisor and/or control room.
>
> Failing to notify others could make you liable under the law. Never ignore a safety or security issue.

Maintain own safety and the safety of other people

The main objective and priority of a steward is safety: personal safety and the safety of everyone else at the event. Always consider carefully what to do if you discover a suspect item that could be a security hazard, and act cautiously. Many items become lost and misplaced at events; the likelihood is that what you have found is legitimate and belongs to someone nearby, but never assume that to be the case – always be cautious.

During the search you will need to be aware of any members of the public in the area and avoid disrupting or alarming them. A calm steward behaving in a professional and confident manner will instil calmness and confidence in the people around them. If there are people in the area you can ask questions, such as, 'Excuse me, does this item belong to you or any of your friends? Can you remember seeing it before?' Their answer will raise, reduce or remove the level of risk in respect of that item.

Report what is found following agreed procedures

You should:

- Communicate verbally and non-verbally with colleagues and other people involved.

- When communicating an incident involving a suspect item, remember that whatever you say is likely to be recorded and used by others to assess the level of response.

- Make sure that any action taken does not risk personal safety and that of other people involved. Always make sure that you assess the risk to yourself and others before dealing with a suspect item.

☐ Report the situation and what you have done clearly and accurately to your supervisor

- get straight to the point (don't waffle!)

- use short, clear wording

- speak slowly

- remain calm

- don't use slang

- be aware of who is listening

- confirm that the supervisor has understood the situation.

The way that you communicate a situation to others can affect their response; failure to communicate an incident clearly could put yourself or others in danger.

Case study

Stardust Ballroom was a nightclub venue in Dublin. On Valentine's Night 1981, the venue caught fire. The fire was discovered behind a curtain. The safety and security staff tried to put it out with fire extinguishers but couldn't. Fire exits had been locked with chains due to a number of burglaries at the venue, causing people to become trapped — 48 teenagers died.

Over to you

☐ How could this disaster have been prevented?

☐ How could you as a steward play an important part in preventing this type of incident?

Best Practice Checklist

How to prepare for a spectator event

☐ Read and understand the Code of Conduct.

☐ Know and understand your roles and responsibilities.

☐ Report in good time and ensure you register your attendance.

☐ Attend the briefing, note important information and read your handbook.

☐ Be clear about the difference between your activities and those of an SIA-licensed operative.

☐ Your standard of appearance and behaviour should be monitored and developed.

☐ Know who to report to and how.

☐ Understand the health and safety signs and know how to check equipment.

☐ Understand how to carry out a search of your designated area and how to tell someone if you find anything suspicious.

☐ Take good care of your resources, including your pass and hand them back after the event.

Working Life

Vijay's story

For the past five years I have been an event steward at my local football club. My team looks after a busy designated area on the terraces behind the goal at the North End.

We get a lot of training, which made me realise how important my job is as we are looking after so many people. One of the things I am really fussy about now is how I search my area. I know the area very well, it's four rows of seats, some steps and the area just behind the goal. Sometimes there are broken seats and occasionally the stairs are wet because the roof leaks when it rains. If I find anything like this I tell my supervisor John and he radios the control room. Within a few minutes someone comes to sort it out.

Last year we had a Code 1, which is a fire report. John said we were on 'yellow patrol', which means 'standby, we may need to evacuate', so we took up our standby positions. My position is on the stairs by the exit, and my role is to make sure that everyone can evacuate safely and calmly without getting hurt. I thought it could be serious because I could smell smoke, but it turned out to be something burning in the kitchen and was dealt with quickly. None of the spectators knew about the problem, the game continued and everyone enjoyed it.

Ask the expert

Q I don't know how I would cope with a really serious situation, especially if the event had to be evacuated.

A You are part of a team and you will be trained in how to deal with these and other situations. You will also be assessed and a supervisor will be there to support you at all times.

Q What should I do if a spectator tells me he has found a bag by his seat which is not his?

A Let your supervisor or control room know so they can decide what to do. Their decision will depend on a number of factors, including intelligence and possibly CCTV recordings.

Do not touch the bag or allow anyone else to touch it (unless the owner claims it). The control room will use the tannoy system to try to trace the owner. If the owner of the bag does not come forward immediately, there will be a procedure to deal with it. In the meantime make sure no one touches the bag and keep everyone away from it.

Top tips

✓ Always act professionally and calmly so as not to cause people to worry or panic.

✓ Know and understand the procedures as well as your roles and responsibilities.

✓ Remember your main responsibility is the safety of the public, your colleagues and yourself.

Check your knowledge

1 State four of the basic legal requirements covering the type of event you are involved in.

2 Why is it important to attend the pre-event briefing?

3 Pre-event routines usually follow a predetermined order. Can you place the following routines in their correct order?

- take position before customer entry
- attend briefing with supervisor or manager
- collect uniform
- sign in/registration
- conduct sweep of venue for hazards/risks
- collect equipment (radio, torch etc.).

4 Why is it important for a steward to wear the correct identification at all times?

5 Describe what sort of hazards you might find when checking the following types of equipment:

- Safety equipment such as a fire extinguisher or your high-visibility jacket
- Security equipment such as a locked exit gate
- Emergency equipment such as a fire emergency exit sign.

6 Why do stewards conduct a pre-event check for hazards and risks?

7 What are the main actions that a steward would be expected to carry out on finding a potential hazard?

8 What do the following signs mean?

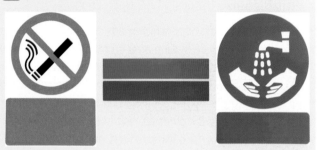

9 What types of hazards might you find in the following areas?

- confined areas
- open areas
- public areas
- non-public areas.

10 What are the most important items to note at the briefing?

Getting ready for assessment

Your assessor will guide you as to when and where assessment will take place, but it will be when you are confident and ready to be assessed. Assessment usually takes place where you work.

Assessment for this unit is about how you prepare for your roles and responsibilities at an event, and will take place more than once at different events. Your assessor will be in the area observing you registering on duty and collecting your resources, such as safety and communication equipment and your stewards' handbook. When you attend the briefing you will make notes of important information, which will be checked to make sure they are correct.

When you are requested to search your area you will be observed and assessed on how well you check and identify physical hazards, as well as the equipment, in a variety

of settings, such as confined, open, public and non-public areas. Your assessor will also assess how well you search different types of areas containing different types of hazards, to be identified by you.

If it is impossible to carry out assessment in your workplace the assessor will design a realistic simulation to cover the following areas:

- identify hazards in your designated area
- follow agreed procedures for assessing risk
- take prompt action appropriate to the hazard and the risk, following agreed procedures and instructions.

Most of the evidence within this unit will be provided by your assessor's observation reports, witness testimony, diaries or reflective accounts, as well as by questions and answers.

Unit 205

Control the entry, exit and movement of people at spectator events

This unit is about controlling and assisting the movement of spectators at events, including their entry to and exit from the venue. You might also be involved in searching people for unauthorised items, such as alcohol, or items that could be used as weapons. This unit therefore also looks at the correct procedure for searching and caring for customers, because this forms a vital part of your role as an event steward.

You will learn how to:

☐ control the entry and exit of people at events

☐ search people for unauthorised items

☐ give people information and help them with other problems.

Control the entry and exit of people at events

Key terms

Resources: the equipment you need to help you in your duties.

Event: any type of public event (for example a sporting event or musical performance).

Venue: the grounds or building where an event takes place.

Emergency: any situation that immediately threatens the health and safety of spectators, staff or yourself (for example, fires or bomb threats).

Resources

There are various **resources** you might need when on duty as an events steward. Some resources are specific to certain types of **event**.

Most event companies will provide basic equipment, but you may need to provide some items yourself. Your company must provide you with health and safety equipment; personal protective equipment (PPE), such as a high-visibility jacket/vest; and some protection against the elements if you will be working outside.

Table 205.1 lists the resources you might need and their purpose. Figure 205.1 shows a typical resources checklist that you might be given for an event.

Resource	Item and purpose
Communications (this could be notebooks for recording incidents, or communications equipment such as radios, if appropriate)	A radio is to maintain contact with your supervisor, control room or colleagues (for example, advising your supervisor of a problem, or being told to search for a suspicious object). A notebook and pen are for you to write down any relevant information
Safety equipment – personal protective equipment (PPE)	Customers need to know who to approach for assistance. The following items of special clothing are designed to make you safe and easily recognisable: • high-visibility vests and jackets • warm clothes • boots • summer clothes. Additional items you might require include: • water • sun cream • torch • disposable gloves • hats • earplugs • waterproofs • gloves • first aid kit.
Safety equipment – in the **venue** (see Pre-event briefing on page 15 in Unit 203)	first aid kit fire alarms assembly points **Emergency** and evacuation plans and procedures Equipment to control the movement of crowds, including barriers, tape, signage, etc.
Keys	Keys are needed to control the entry and exit gate in your area.
Handbook (issued to you at the pre-event briefing, see Unit 203 page 13)	A handbook tells you what to do in various situations. The handbook should be issued at your briefing, before the event. It should contain information about the event, the venue, and your roles and responsibilities. It should also contain security and safety procedures (evacuation plans, venue regulations, layout and a map of the venue). A map of key points at the venue is required so you can find your way around the site. A timetable of events shows you what is happening and when.

Table 205.1: Resources and their purpose

Resource	Received (signature)	Returned (signature)
Stewards' handbook		
Keys		
Notebook and pens		To be retained by the steward
Radio		
High-visibility vest and/or jacket		
Boots		
Water		
Disposable gloves		
Waterproof jacket and trousers		
Hat		
Gloves		
Torch		
Earplugs		
First aid kit		

Figure 205.1 An example of a resources checklist

When you have been given your equipment, you will need to check it. Before you sign for it, you need to make sure that everything is working properly and is fit for purpose. For example, turn the radio on, select the correct frequency, speak into it to send a test message and listen to the reply. Look through the handbook, so that you know what is in it. Write down any key information in your notebook.

Functional skills

English: reading and writing — Checking your resources against a checklist will help you develop your English skills in reading and writing.

Think about it

What type of PPE might you require as an event steward at:

a) a rugby match in November?

b) a music festival in summer?

Make sure you've got appropriate equipment

Standards of behaviour and appearance

You need to be immediately identifiable as a steward so wear the correct uniform at all times. This includes your high-visibility vest and your identification badge. Customers will then know they can approach you if they have any questions or problems.

- Look and act like a professional. It should be clear that you are in control of the situation.

- Be calm and assertive, but not aggressive. The spectators need be able to approach you if they want information or have a problem. Try to make them feel at ease by matching your words, tone and **body language** to the customer's. Treat them equally and with respect.

- Use safety equipment to control the entry and exit of people. For example, you can use signs, barriers, steward cordons and loud speakers (if necessary and appropriate).

- **Actively listen.**

- Check understanding.

- Create empathy – **communicate** with the customers so you can understand each other's point of view.

- Work towards establishing trust; by doing so you will de-escalate any situation and identify a positive outcome for both sides (win–win).

Standards of behaviour and appearance are covered in more detail in Unit 203 page 2.

Greet people

When the public first see you at a venue, you must use your customer care skills well. You want their visit to the event to be pleasant and enjoyable.

Make the people in the queue feel welcome. Greet them in a friendly manner. Ask how you can help in a courteous, non-threatening, way, for example, 'How can I help you, Sir/Madam?' Take responsibility for any enquiry made to you and do all you can to resolve the issue. Try to maintain a positive, 'can-do' attitude throughout your conversation.

You will be dealing with all types people at an event, who will have many different problems. They are your customers, so deal with their problems, or provide them with the information they have requested, with courtesy and respect.

In a conversation, active listening is a very valuable skill and you will need to practise doing this well.

- Listen to the actual words and check with the speaker to make sure that you understand what their needs are. If you listen properly to your customer, you will look much more professional and you will be able to do your job more effectively.

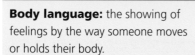

Key terms

Body language: the showing of feelings by the way someone moves or holds their body.

Active listening: showing that you are paying attention to what someone is saying, for example, by maintaining eye contact, nodding, asking further questions.

Communicate: by using words, as well as body language, tone of voice, etc.

☐ Concentrate on the person and try not to be distracted by what is going on around you. Let them know that you are listening and encourage them to continue, by acknowledging what they are saying.

☐ You may need to ask questions, or even summarise, to clarify what they have said.

☐ You need to show the speaker that you have been listening, you do understand their issues and you are willing to solve their problem.

Designated area

At an event you are a member of a team with responsibility for a specific, or designated, area, where you will be positioned.

Some common **designated areas**, where stewards are usually placed, are:

☐ car parks

☐ ticket barriers

☐ gates

☐ turnstiles

☐ the box office

☐ queue control barriers.

When you arrive at your designated area, you will need to:

☐ check the area to ensure it is safe (for example, no wet floors or dangerous wiring)

☐ check that the safety equipment is in place (for example, fire extinguishers and first aid boxes), that the turnstiles and toilets are working properly, that fire exit lights and doors are functioning, and that the exit door chains and locks have been removed and doors will open in an emergency

☐ search the area to ensure there are no suspicious packages.

If your designated area is an entry or exit point for a venue, you will have specific roles to perform. For example, you might be required to:

☐ meet and greet people

☐ check tickets

☐ send people to the appropriate area (e.g. VIP area or specific stands)

☐ search people

☐ refuse entry to people.

Admitting and refusing entry

The entry and exit procedures will vary depending on the type of event.

A football match will have queues, turnstiles and ticketed entry. People may start to arrive up to two hours before kick-off and allowed to enter the grounds at

Key term

Designated area: the area you are responsible for.

this point. The exit from a football event is usually much quicker – it might take only 30 minutes for everyone to leave the venue itself. However, it will probably take them much longer to leave the car parks and surrounding areas, due to congestion.

However, a large exhibition centre might have a constant stream of people arriving throughout the day and exiting at various times. There are often few people left at the end of the day at an exhibition centre, so there is unlikely to be much congestion in the car park.

How would you deal with this type of situation and its potential risks?

Most people who attend an event arrive in good spirits and are there to enjoy the occasion. Even so, everyone will have different needs. It is best to maintain a calm but authoritative manner when dealing with the public, but you will need to adapt your style depending on the type of person and the situation you are dealing with (as shown in Table 205.2). Some people may see an event as an opportunity to commit offences or behave unsociably.

The safety and security of all people who attend or work at an event is paramount. There are often standards and rules to govern what people can and cannot do within a venue, and there will also be restrictions on what objects they can bring.

If your role at an event is to control the entry of people, you will need to know the rules and procedures for entry to that particular venue. These procedures might involve asking people to leave certain property in an office until they leave (e.g. cameras) or confiscating other property (such as fireworks, flares, smoke canisters, knives, bottles, glasses, cans, poles) and any other items that could compromise public safety.

Football grounds have strict regulations set by the Football Licensing Authority relating to people who attempt to enter with any of these unauthorised items. Unless you are a steward at a football club and have been specifically tasked to eject people, this role must be left to someone licensed under the Private Security Industry Act, for example, an SIA-licensed door supervisor.

Type of people	How to deal with them
Friendly, excited, cooperative	Match their energy, attitude and behaviour
Uncooperative, unfriendly	Actively listen and empathise
Emotional	De-escalate the situation – dynamic risk assessment
Intoxicated	Assertive with humour (dynamic risk assessment) May need to refuse entry (depending on level of intoxication)
With particular needs	Maintain a professional approach – treat in the same way as anyone else but take account of their needs. For example, you will need to sort out access and egress for a wheelchair user. Talk at their height level and use eye contact. Take the lead from that person or their carer and ask how you can assist rather than making assumptions
VIPs	Maintain a professional approach – treat in the same way as anyone else, depending on the type of person.
With limited understanding of English	Actively listen, check their understanding, and be patient

Table 205.2 Different types of people and how to deal with them

The safety of the people at the event is at risk

Key terms

Monitoring: keeping a careful eye on a situation.

Colleagues: the people you work with (those working at your own level and your managers).

Entries and exits at venues should be carefully monitored at all times to ensure both your safety and the safety of the public. **Monitoring** is carried out by your **colleagues** and by those who work in the control room. The control room may be observing your area using closed circuit television cameras (CCTV).

Event venues are private property, unless the event is taking place in a public place such as a street. The venue owners and the organisers and promoters of the event will produce procedures to outline how people should behave.

There are various laws that cover trespassing on private property and these may be reflected in your work as follows:

- ☐ Only customers in possession of a valid ticket will be admitted into the venue.
- ☐ Lost, stolen or damaged tickets will not be replaced.
- ☐ Tickets are non-refundable and non-transferable.
- ☐ Licensing laws are strictly enforced.
- ☐ Ticket holders may be subject to search.
- ☐ No bottles, cans, alcohol or food (including bottled water) are to be brought into the venue.
- ☐ No illegal substances may be brought into the venue. Anyone found in possession of any illegal substance or item will be refused entry/ejected from the venue and may be reported to the police.
- ☐ Anyone found in possession of a weapon may be refused entry/ejected and the item seized and handed to the police.
- ☐ CCTV cameras are in operation at this venue.

These laws are the basis on which authorised people (who act on behalf of the organisers) are able to refuse entry or eject those who do not comply with the conditions of entry. When attending an event, visitors are agreeing to the conditions that apply to it. This is the law of contract. To prevent confusion and possible conflict, customers should know about conditions of entry before they arrive at an event; these are often printed on the ticket and on a website.

When enforcing relevant legislation, you should always seek the customer's cooperation first. A firm, but polite, approach must be used at all times. The words 'please' and 'thank you' should be the ones used most in this situation.

Sometimes people will attempt to enter an event illegally (usually to avoid payment). Some of the most common methods are outlined below.

Key term

Unauthorised entrance: an entrance that has not been approved.

They may use **unauthorised entrances**. Entry into any event is through an approved and easily recognisable entrance, which will usually involve queues and stewards checking tickets and bags. Sometimes people will attempt to gain entry to an event via an unauthorised route such as a hole or by jumping over a fence. These people need to be ejected. Under such circumstances, you should inform a supervisor immediately and report as many details of the person as possible (for example, height, clothes, direction travelled). People may also attempt to gain unauthorised entrance by using one of the following methods.

- Offering an incentive such as money or gifts — this is a criminal act and you should report it to your supervisor immediately.

- Forged or duplicate tickets — if you think a ticket or pass is forged or a copy, you should inform your supervisor. The event managers or box office will decide whether or not the ticket is genuine and whether to allow admission.

- Forced entry — once again, this is a criminal act, which may require police involvement. If this happens, contact your supervisor immediately.

If a decision is made to exclude people from an event, you will be expected to know and understand the relevant legislation and organisational policy. There are usually a number of options, depending on the circumstances. These include:

- giving a verbal warning

- refusing admission

- ejection from the event

- detention and possible arrest/police assistance.

In order to eject somebody, in most cases you will need a SIA (Security Industry Act) licence, as this activity can be classed as door supervision or acting as a security guard. Always ensure that you are aware of the legal requirements for refusing entry or asking someone to leave, and your powers as a steward at the events you deal with.

If someone needs to be asked to leave a venue, inform your supervisor as you are not authorised to eject people

Explain reasons for refusing entry

If you need to refuse a person entry to an event, give an explanation for refusing admission and involve your supervisor. Always draw the customer's attention to the conditions of entry or relevant information (usually contained on the printed ticket). For example, the back of the ticket could say that the venue places great importance on the safety of its customers and can only allow entry to visitors who are willing to comply. Do not allow the refusal to become personal. Remain calm, even if the customer becomes antagonistic.

Reasons for refusal to admit to the venue might include the following:

- for health and safety reasons no further admissions to the venue can take place as the capacity of the venue has been reached
- the ticket holder has been acting in an inappropriate way in the vicinity of the venue and may pose a risk to their own safety or the safety and enjoyment of others at the venue
- the ticket holder is using abusive language or is threatening violence towards others at the venue.

Functional skills

English: speaking and listening – When you communicate with customers, take the time to understand their requests and respond to them in an appropriate manner. This will allow you to develop your English speaking skills.

Case study

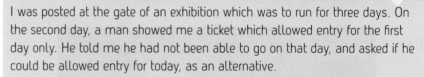

I was posted at the gate of an exhibition which was to run for three days. On the second day, a man showed me a ticket which allowed entry for the first day only. He told me he had not been able to go on that day, and asked if he could be allowed entry for today, as an alternative.

I explained to him that if I allowed him entry there might be a safety problem as the organisers would not know who was in the exhibition hall if there was an emergency. I offered to take him to the box office to see if they would exchange his ticket.

Over to you

- How would you have dealt with this customer?
- What might have happened if you told the customer there was nothing you could do because he had the wrong ticket, and refused him entry?

Control queues

Any event that requires stewards is likely to have queues. The more people there are, the longer they will have to wait and the less inclined they will be to wait patiently. They may jostle each other, surge forward when turnstiles are opened, or try to seek other entry points.

Your job as a steward is to make sure that you manage the queues properly, which will reduce the likelihood of problems arising. People waiting in queues are customers, so you must treat them with consideration.

☐ Use safety equipment to manage queues (e.g. signs, barriers, steward cordons, etc).

☐ Keep everyone informed of what is happening and updated regularly. Always behave in a professional manner.

☐ Be calm and assertive, but not aggressive. Match words, tone and body language.

The venue will be equipped with access-control systems to assist with controlling queues.

Table 205.3 outlines the types of equipment used to control queues and how they are used in a venue.

Type of equipment	How it is used
Filter cordon	A line of stewards (and/or police) who face the approaching crowd, check tickets and identify people to search at random, or with suspicion
Barrier cordon	A line of stewards (and/or police) who form a physical barrier in order to contain and direct people as they move
Notices	To provide information about entry conditions
Signs	Signs are placed in advance of a queue, to direct people to the appropriate gate (depending on the type of ticket they have)

Table 205.3 Resources for managing queues

Badly managed queues can often be the first point of tension and frustration, especially when there are delays to an event's scheduled opening time, and are often due to a lack of experience and/or lack of planning and preparation. There may have been incorrect information about the type or number of people coming to the event. Here is an example of how a straightforward event can turn into a real problem.

Case study

I was at the opening of a new department store in the city centre and the store's marketing department had advertised the event on TV, radio, internet and local papers. There were a number of special offers – some real bargains for people who could get in first! An event company and the police were involved in the planning and risk assessment, but they completely underestimated the number of people who turned up.

Just before the store was due to open, hundreds of people arrived all at once. The police called for reinforcements, due to the risk of people being crushed, but it was too late. The pressure of people pushing and shoving from behind, with nowhere to go at the front of the queue, led to injuries. It even damaged the structure of the store.

Over to you

☐ How would you deal with this situation?

☐ How could this situation have been avoided?

Skills builder

Examine the ways in which other members of your team deal with customers. If possible ask your supervisor or an experienced steward to observe you dealing with a customer's problems and feed back to you afterwards.

● Why is body language such an important part of the way you communicate with people?

● How can you practise being assertive without sounding aggressive?

Unit 205

Control the entry, exit and movement of people at spectator events

Risk assessments should take into account the number of people expected at an event. How would you deal with a queue surge like this?

Supervise the safe exit of spectators

Once the event is over (and sometimes before the end of the event) people will start to leave. This process needs to be managed and controlled carefully. The main priority for the exit at any event is to make sure that people leave safely. The safe exit of people from a venue will form a major part of any event's **risk** assessment and safety plan.

Your part in the exit strategy will depend on where your designated area is and your procedures and role in the event. For example, if you are positioned at a gate or in a car parking area, your role will be totally different from that of a colleague who is involved in stewarding the 'pit' area during a music event.

To ensure that everyone leaves the venue safely, you will need to check your designated area to ensure that there are no obstacles on the exit route. For example:

- Ensure all exits are clear of obstructions that could interrupt or stop the flow of spectators (to avoid crushing).

- Open gates in plenty of time to ensure a smooth passage of people.

- Make sure there is nothing in the way that could lead to trips, slips or falls, which could halt the steady flow of people as well as causing injury.

- If your designated area is in the car park, make sure that pedestrians are separated from moving vehicles.

Key term

Risk: the likelihood of a hazard causing harm and the seriousness of this harm.

The car park is a dangerous place. A lot of people will be trying to get home and many will be impatient. At any given time during the exit stage, you could have:

- cars trying to leave the car park
- people walking across the car park, to get to their cars
- pedestrians walking across the car park as a short cut
- drivers trying to find alternative exits.

An event may have to be evacuated in an emergency. You need a clear understanding of what to do to ensure everyone gets out safely. The emergency evacuation procedure will be covered in your pre-event briefing and in your steward's handbook.

Inform your supervisor about problems

You may be approached by a person with a problem, or you might see a problem and go over to offer assistance. In any case, you should always try to resolve the issue yourself. However, there may be occasions where you need to involve your supervisor if the problem is something beyond your role (for example, first aid).

It is extremely important that you never leave your designated area in order to deal with a problem, unless you receive a specific instruction to do so. You will have been placed in a designated area so that the venue can comply with health and safety requirements. You can contact your supervisor by:

- speaking to them directly, if you are working in a small team and your supervisor is nearby
- radioing the control room to request that the supervisor comes over to you
- radioing your supervisor directly.

Once the supervisor arrives in your area, you need to explain what the problem is. You can seek their advice, or hand over the problem to them. In some cases, you might need to ask another responsible person for help, for example:

- if the customer has sustained an injury, you will need a first aider
- if someone has gained entry illegally, you will need a security officer
- if you suspect that an offence (e.g. assault or theft) has been committed, you will need a police officer.

Always keep the customer informed. They will want to know what is happening and who will be coming to help them.

Best Practice Checklist

How you should care for your customers

- Always act professionally.
- Look smart, friendly and approachable.
- Show respect for everyone.
- Treat all customers equally.
- Actively listen and always check understanding.
- Know your organisation's policies and procedures, the Code of Conduct and the limits of your authority.
- Establish empathy and understanding.
- Seek assistance from colleagues when necessary.
- Always seek a win–win situation when appropriate.
- Learn from experience.

Search people for unauthorised items

Identify people to be searched

The most important thing to remember is that you have no right to search anyone. You must always ask for and obtain someone's permission before carrying out a search. This is true even if it clearly states on the ticket or on a sign at the entry that there is a search policy at the venue. It is good practice that you should only search people who are the same sex as you.

You should never search anyone without knowing the venue's search policy. This covers things such as:

- the list of prohibited items (items not allowed at the venue)
- the need to obtain permission before searching anyone
- the need for same-sex searches
- how to handle and confiscate property
- the procedure for confiscated items and their return after the event.

Remember:

- never handle anyone or their property without permission
- the right of admission to a venue may be subject to a search
- no one is exempt from the search policy (not even the manager or VIPs)
- always remain polite and courteous and thank people after the search.

> **Remember:** Risk assessments can change. Even during an event, the audience profile can change and in this case the search procedure will need to change as well.

Your venue will have its own procedures on how to identify people who need to be searched as they enter. For example, searches may be carried out at random, unless it is suspected that a particular person or group of people are in possession of illegal, prohibited or unauthorised items (from that person's demeanour or because of information or intelligence). Alternatively, it may be a condition of entry that spectators allow themselves (and their belongings) to be searched by qualified and trained staff at the entrance.

Searching with or without a licence

Whether you are involved in searching will depend on a variety of circumstances, including:

- the licensing conditions of the venue
- whether you are licensed by the SIA
- the risk assessment for the event
- the type of event.

In England and Wales, you could be exempt from being required to have a SIA licence if you are an in-house employee carrying out your duties in a certified sports ground or stadium, which is covered by a valid and current safety certificate. Always make sure of your legal powers as a steward at your venue before carrying out a search.

Body searches can only be carried out by someone who holds a current SIA licence

It is worth highlighting what the law says is **licensable activity**. The SIA provide some useful guidance on their website. Please see www.pearsonhotlinks.co.uk, search for this title and select this unit number. For example, you will usually require a licence if the activity you are carrying out involves:

- manned guarding activity
- door supervision
- public space surveillance (CCTV)
- close protection
- key holding
- cash and valuables.

Screening or searching people entering premises (or their subsequent removal) is a licensable activity, since you are guarding against one or more of the activities listed in paragraph 2 (1) of Schedule 2 of the Private Security Industry Act. If you are given responsibility for searching people or bags, you will require a licence as a steward to do your job.

Key term

Licensable activity: a licensable activity is determined by the role that is performed and the activity undertaken. These are described fully in Section 3 and Schedule 2 of the Private Security Industry Act 2001 (as amended).

However, there are exceptions to this rule. For example, if you are employed as a steward by the venue (rather than by an external contractor) your employer may allow you to search spectators under what is called 'common law and the law of contract'. It is extremely important that you always check your venue's search policy as it affects your role as a steward before undertaking any search. Checking that people have paid for admission (or have invitations or passes allowing admission) before they enter the venue does not require a licence.

Other licensable activities

If you are faced with a sudden or unexpected situation, such as a fight, or if you need to help a colleague who is being attacked by members of the crowd, you do not need a licence to deal with the situation. However, it is your responsibility, and your employer's, to carry a licence if the requirement to respond to such incidents is included in your job description, or if you will be involved in ejecting individuals.

If you do not have the correct and appropriate licence and you carry out a licensable activity it is a criminal offence.

Volunteers

A volunteer is not employed or contracted, and therefore not licensable under the Private Security Act 2001. If you are a volunteer, you must receive no financial benefit, payment in kind or reward for your services.

Ask for permission to search

You will always have to ask for permission to search a person. Remember to be polite, professional and positive.

Most people attending an event will understand why they are being searched and will cooperate fully. Occasionally, people will refuse to be searched. When this happens, remind them of the reason why they are being searched (that it is a condition of entry) and then ask again if they mind. This job is all about communication skills, so you need to explain clearly and politely why you need to conduct a search. If there are any further refusals, you will need to speak to your supervisor immediately — you must never forcibly search anyone.

Think about it

You are a female steward who is part of a search team at one of the entrances. You are working with the search team because you have an SIA licence as a Door Supervisor. Everyone is being searched before they enter the venue. A man approaches the entrance and comes towards you. What would you do?

Best Practice Checklist

Carrying out a personal search

- ☐ Always ask permission to search.

- ☐ Only search people of the same sex as yourself.

- ☐ Be sensitive to people's feelings (people can be offended or embarrassed).

- ☐ Only search outer garments.

- ☐ Always ask the person to turn out their own pockets or empty the contents of their bag(s) onto a table.

- ☐ Know what to do if you find prohibited or unlawful items.

- ☐ Always be aware of your own personal safety – beware of sharp objects such as needles, razor blades etc.

- ☐ Use the backs of your hands to feel for objects when searching outer garments.

- ☐ Keep your body facing to the side of the person being searched: this reduces the opportunity for the person to assault you.

- ☐ Work systematically from top to toe.

- ☐ Know your organisation's policy and procedure.

- ☐ Work in teams and/or in view of CCTV so you always have witnesses.

Who you can search

You must always follow the venue's **policies** and **procedures** and only search people of the same sex as yourself, male on male, female on female. Be aware also of any privacy and equality issues that could arise. People with disabilities may be accompanied by carers who may assist in the search, bearing in mind that 'search' only relates to outer garments and bags. It is also important for anyone with a disability to let the searcher know they have a disability, for example, a person who is unable to raise their arm should let the searcher know they would find this uncomfortable. There should also be other options, such as a private area to perform the search, or different types of help and support. A typical 'search' will only take a few seconds, but searching people is always a sensitive area – it is intrusive and personal, and people can easily become offended and embarrassed. Be careful to follow procedures and take care of your own personal safety. There must be colleagues working with you whenever you are involved in searching people. Supervisors usually observe searching procedures to check that the procedures are carried out correctly.

Key terms

Policies: what an organisation says its staff should and should not do in certain situations.

Procedures: a way of carrying out policies as part of an activity or process.

Think about it

a) How would you search someone in a wheelchair?

b) How would you search a child?

Procedures for dealing with unauthorised items

Key term

Prohibited items: items not allowed into venues under any circumstances.

Be aware that there are occasions when you will find **prohibited items** – items not allowed into venues under any circumstances and covered by various regulations. This list of unauthorised items will vary from venue to venue but may include:

- alcohol
- illegal drugs
- offensive weapons (could be knives, bottles, flares and many other items)
- glass containers
- any bottle or container with a top on it
- fireworks
- flares
- smoke canisters
- laser pens
- poles
- dogs (except for guide dogs)
- cameras.

You need to find out from your venue what to do if you find an unauthorised object or prohibited item. There will be an organisational policy which covers this and you will probably have various options, depending on the nature of the item. For example:

- a camera may be confiscated and kept in an office until after the event has finished
- items that could compromise public safety (e.g. fireworks, flares, smoke canisters, knives etc.) may be confiscated, or you could ask the person to put the item elsewhere (e.g. locked away in their car)
- anyone found in possession of particularly dangerous items may be refused entry, ejected from the venue, arrested or detained by the police.

If any person attempting to enter the venue is in possession of unlawful items you must inform your supervisor, who will then decide what to do with the item and its owner.

Treat people with courtesy and respect

- Be polite and courteous at all times, and always treat customers with respect.
- Show respect for people's property when carrying out a search.

52

What would you do if you notice someone carrying any unauthorised and/or illegal items?

☐ Remember that you are one person in a team and that your colleagues also have roles and responsibilities within the team.

☐ Follow health and safety procedures, remembering your personal safety and the use of PPE.

☐ Should you find anything suspicious, unauthorised or prohibited, you must be aware of the procedures regarding these items.

☐ Always finish the search by thanking the person.

Practise the following sentences.

☐ 'Excuse me Sir/Madam, would you mind showing me what is in your bag, please?'

☐ 'Would you mind emptying your pockets on the table, please?'

☐ 'Would you mind telling me what is in this bottle/bag/box, please?'

☐ 'I'm really sorry, I see you have a camera with you. This venue does not allow cameras to be taken inside, but you can leave it in the property office. We will look after it for you, give you a receipt and you will be able to collect it after the show.'

Key term

Conflict: situations in which people disagree strongly, which may lead to violence or other forms of unlawful or unsociable behaviour.

There is always the possibility that someone will refuse to be searched, or have objections to being searched. This may lead to **conflict** where the situation may escalate very rapidly. You will need to know how to use conflict management and communication skills to de-escalate a situation and resolve the problem to the satisfaction of all parties.

De-escalation methods include:

- active listening
- being assertive, not aggressive
- pointing out the consequences of non-compliance and checking mutual understanding
- seeking a win–win outcome.

Skills builder

If you are involved in searching people before they are allowed to enter an event, you must make sure that you know the organisation's search policy and procedure. If you are new to the venue, or have never carried out searching before:

- ask your supervisor for a copy of the organisation's search policy and procedure. If there is anything you don't understand, ask them to explain it to you
- watch how the experienced members of a search team carry out their work
- try to work with a colleague who is experienced at searching people so you can learn from them and have their support when you first conduct a search.

Give people information and help them with other problems

Communicating with people

At any venue or event there will be many different types of people, including:

- cooperative
- uncooperative
- intoxicated
- emotional
- people with limited understanding of English
- VIPs (Very Important People)
- people with **particular needs**.

Key term

Particular needs: the needs, for example, of disabled people, elderly people or children.

Each of these people will have their own requirements. You will need to know how to act appropriately and **impartially** at all times, remaining professional and courteous.

How you communicate with people is very important. If you do not communicate clearly, you could direct someone to the wrong location, or upset or anger a customer. You need to:

☐ actively listen and empathise

☐ carry out a dynamic risk assessment throughout the process and try to de-escalate any problems before they become unmanageable

☐ be assertive, but remember that humour often helps

☐ show patience, check mutual understanding and sum up what has been said

☐ act professionally, no matter who you are dealing with

☐ be willing and able to assist people with particular needs.

When communicating with people with particular needs, take your lead from them or their carers. For example, when speaking to a child or young person, or a wheelchair user, come down to their level.

Always try to remain visible and approachable: you need to be available to speak to customers. If you see someone who looks confused or lost, it is good practice to go to them and ask if they need assistance.

Dealing with a customer's problem

You will encounter a range of problems at different events. For example, you may have to deal with ticketing problems, lost property, missing people, unsociable or unlawful behaviour, or complaints/suggestions about the facility and its procedures. You need to know the venue's policies and procedures for dealing with problems.

> ### Think about it
>
> A couple tell you that when they arrived at the event they were carrying a bag containing their wallet with credit cards and some money, which is now missing. They know they had the bag when they stopped for coffee about 20 minutes ago, but they cannot remember what happened to it after that. What would you do?
>
> You will need to actively listen to them and make the following enquiries:
>
> - Ask them where the coffee shop is and where they have been since then.
> - Check the time they were there, what the bag looked like, and what it contained.
> - Find out their personal and contact details.
> - Make a record of the incident.
> - Communicate the information to your supervisor or control room.

Always ensure that you have the full picture. Without this, you (or anyone else) cannot make an informed decision and it may lead to confusion.

Key term

Impartial: not favouring or discriminating against any particular type of person.

Functional skills

English: speaking and listening – By listening to customers' problems and communicating with them in a clear way you will be developing your English skills in speaking and listening.

Never enter into an argument with a customer. The customer has a problem and it is your responsibility to help them. Some customers may swear, intimidate and threaten. Think of the most effective way of solving the problem, quickly. Listen and find out exactly what the customer wants – this shows interest and concern. Allow the customer to finish, even if they are angry. They may simply need an outlet to vent their frustrations and if you are able to remain calm, you could help to avert a potentially high-emotion situation.

If you think you are getting into difficulties, contact your supervisor.

Think about it

● Why do you think it is important to keep people informed about how their problem or complaint is being dealt with?

● How would you feel if you reported a problem and no one came back to you with an answer?

Refer to other people

If you are unable to solve a customer's problem, you may need to refer the customer to:

- ☐ your supervisor
- ☐ a colleague
- ☐ an information point
- ☐ the police.

Always refer to your supervisor or control room if you're not sure how to deal with a situation

You are part of a team. If you don't know which person to refer to, ask a colleague, your supervisor or control room or someone at an information point, so that an answer can be provided quickly and efficiently. If you need to hand a problem on, introduce the customer to whoever will be helping them next and make sure both parties understand the situation fully.

Best Practice Checklist

Helping people with problems

☐ Always communicate with people politely and clearly.

☐ Listen attentively and actively at all times.

☐ Be professional: first impressions are very important.

☐ Ask if you can help and remain visible and approachable.

☐ Be aware of a person's particular needs.

☐ Ensure that you are always impartial.

☐ Never argue with anyone and get help from a supervisor if you are getting into difficulties.

☐ Always try to get as much information as possible: find out exactly what the problem is and check your understanding.

☐ Communicate with the person regularly and let them know what you are doing to help them with the problem.

Ask for information

Customers will often ask you for information about an event or venue. For example, a person may ask you where a particular gate is, or they may be looking for a toilet or the beer tent. You need to be able to answer their questions as quickly and efficiently as possible.

You should have received most of the basic information you need during the briefing, or it may appear in your steward's handbook or in the event programme. You should have a map of the venue showing the location of the main facilities and key points (such as gates and evacuation points). You will also need to know where to find facilities such as first aid posts, the lost property office, lifts, refreshments, hospitality areas, prayer rooms and so on.

Be aware that there is some information you should not provide to customers (usually relating to security and data protection). This type of information will be outlined in the venue's policy, but if you are unsure, ask a supervisor.

Think about it

What sort of questions might customers ask you? How can you find the answers before you are asked? Where is the relevant information?

Security

Never provide people with information which could compromise security of the venue or the people at the event. This could include:

☐ code words

☐ pass codes

☐ event intelligence, such as the VIPs attending

☐ details of incidents (past or present)

☐ the location of offices, the control room, or backstage details.

Data protection

Never provide anyone with information which is personal to people or could lead to them being identified. This could include names and addresses or contact details of staff, colleagues or supervisors.

Dealing with complaints

It is always important to be positive and create the right climate when dealing with a potential or actual complaint. Actively listen to the person. If the complaint cannot be immediately resolved, refer to a supervisor. Make sure that you follow the venue's policies and procedures for complaint handling and reporting (they will have been explained to you at the pre-event briefing).

Depending on your role at the event, the complaint could be received verbally and passed on to the control room or supervisor to deal with, or you may be involved in formally receiving and recording the complaint yourself. If you need to record a complaint formally, you should:

☐ acknowledge the customer's complaint

☐ know where to locate any complaint forms

☐ know who to send the completed complaint form to

☐ be aware of any reporting procedures that you need to make in the event of a complaint.

Case study

I work in a large arena where I direct people to their seats and make sure that fire exits are always kept clear. One evening a spectator approached to say he had a ticket to an area of the event where there was hardly any view of the stage. He said he had paid a lot of money to get into the venue, only to find out that he couldn't see anything and wanted to complain to the organiser.

It was very difficult to see the stage from that position and I could immediately empathise with the customer, but it was not my role to try to resolve the problem. I have an important job to do and it would be unsafe for me to move from my position.

Over to you

- ☐ What would you do if you received a complaint such as this?

- ☐ What would you advise the customer to do?

- ☐ What information would you need to obtain from the customer before informing your supervisor or control room?

Skills builder

If customers have a complaint you should know what the procedure is. The venue's policy will be explained to you by your supervisor and during the pre-event briefing.

- Always listen very carefully to a person making a complaint and check with them that you understand the issue.

- If you cannot deal with the problem immediately, inform your supervisor.

- If possible, observe your supervisor when they deal with a complaint and use this experience as best practice.

- Ask if you can see a complaint form so that you know what details are required before you need to complete it.

Take account of diversity and equality issues at spectator events

It is important in your professional behaviour and care of customers that you take into account the **diversity** and **equality** of all people, and do not exercise any **discrimination**. It is not necessary for someone to prove that you actually intended to discriminate against them. It is sufficient to say that as a result of your actions that person received less favourable treatment.

Some factors to take account of include:

- age
- ethnic group: the group you belong to which shares a common culture
- religion
- beliefs, attitudes and values: things you believe in, such as your political or religious beliefs
- gender: male/female
- race: a person's national origin and/or colour
- disability: covers a wide range of requirements that people may have, including:
  - learning
  - physical or mental
  - developmental
  - short term
  - permanent.

Remember that you represent the venue as well as your company. You will find that the company and venue you work for will include equality, diversity and discrimination in their policies and procedures. Look for signs of this around the venue, such as:

- evacuation routes and procedures for people who have physical disabilities
- wheelchair access and viewing areas
- access ramps and routes around the venue
- toilets and other facilities
- lifts
- large print materials
- prayer rooms
- speakers in certain areas for people with hearing impairments
- a range of food products.

Key terms

Diversity: is about valuing everyone as an individual. People are not alike, and everyone has their own tastes, needs, personality, culture, beliefs and behaviours.

Equality: is when everyone is treated equally, regardless of their differences in age, gender, race, religion or belief, ethnic origin, sexual orientation, gender reassignment and disability.

Discrimination: the unfair treatment of a person or a group, on the basis of prejudice.

Working Life

George's story

I decided to be an event steward five years ago because I love going to gigs and there was a good music venue near where I lived. My first role after being accepted was as part of a team positioned at the main entrance. At my first gig there was a big group of lads who arrived together. Most of them presented their tickets with no problem, but one claimed he had lost his on the way to the venue. I didn't know what to do because it was my first day on the job, so I called my supervisor over to help me. I explained the situation and my supervisor said that the only thing to do was for him to buy a new ticket if there were any available. I showed him where the box office was, and he bought a new ticket and got to see his favourite band with the rest of his mates. Once I had seen how my supervisor had dealt with it, I felt confident I would be able to deal with a similar situation myself the next time.

Ask the expert

Q What should I do if there's a situation I don't know how to handle?

A Let your supervisor or the control room know, so they can advise you or deal with it.

Q What should I do if the customer does not speak English?

A Let your supervisor or control room know so they can find someone who can speak their language. Try to reassure the customer by smiling and using your body language.

Top tips

✓ Never try to deal with a problem that falls outside your remit, or that you do not feel confident with.

✓ Know when you should ask your supervisor for help.

✓ Always keep the customer informed if you are handing them over to someone else.

Check your knowledge

1 Why is it important to wear the correct identification?

2 What could be the result of a poorly managed queue?

3 Why is it important that you clearly and politely explain to someone why you are refusing them entry?

4 Why is it important to monitor your designated area carefully?

5 Why must you only search people of the same sex as yourself?

6 What are the correct methods of carrying out personal searches?

7 Why is it important to provide people with proper explanations and treat them with courtesy?

8 How would you communicate with the following types of people?
- cooperative
- uncooperative
- intoxicated
- emotional
- with limited understanding of English.

9 Why is it important to get all the relevant information before you try to solve a problem?

10 Who should you refer problems to when you cannot deal with them yourself?

Getting ready for assessment

Once you have had some experience of controlling the entry and exit of people at spectator events, and feel confident, you are ready to be assessed for this unit.

You will have to prove that you have the correct resources at all times, are competent at controlling the entry and exit of people at events, and are able to deal with different types of customers. You should be able to demonstrate the correct method of searching, provide people with information and help them with problems.

You should look at each learning outcome and be prepared for the following types of assessment.

Be prepared to show the assessor the resources that you have with you, for example communications, safety equipment, your handbook and perhaps keys. The assessor will observe how you meet and greet different types of people, admit or refuse entry, provide people with reasons

why they have been refused entry, and supervise people as they leave the event.

You will also be assessed if you are involved in searching people as they enter the event. Your assessor will look at how you identify people to search, ask for permission, treat customers with courtesy and respect, carry out the search using the correct procedure and inform your supervisor about any unlawful items that you find.

Please note that if you do not get involved in any of the above procedures (usually because you do not have an SIA licence), your assessor will design a realistic scenario so you can be observed carrying out these procedures.

At all times your assessor will make sure that you are able to communicate with people and that you can deal with their problems or complaints.

Unit 206

Monitor spectators and deal with crowd problems

This unit is about monitoring crowds and groups of spectators to make sure that any issues such as local overcrowding, over-capacity, unexpected crowd movements, or people engaging in unsociable or unlawful behaviour, are noticed early and can be dealt with. The unit will help you to recognise signs of potential problems and you will learn how to respond without placing yourself or others at risk. This unit will also tell you which resources you will need to perform your role, and give you information and procedures to enable you to carry out your role effectively.

You will learn how to:
- monitor crowds and identify potential problems
- follow instructions and procedures to deal with crowd problems.

Monitor crowds and identify potential problems

Resources

In Unit 203, you looked at the resources you will need for your role as an event steward, including the need to wear your identification. This needs to be clearly visible because it identifies you as a person in authority who can give assistance and advice. It is a condition of employment that you can be identified as a steward at all times when you are on duty.

For this learning outcome, you will also need the appropriate **communications resources**, such as a radio to communicate with your supervisor and/or the control room.

Appropriate behaviour and appearance

Your behaviour and appearance must be professional and must meet the standards required by your employer and by the owners or promoters of the **event**. In any large crowd situation there is a risk of potential problems. It is the responsibility of stewards to deal with such situations in a calm and controlled manner, in order to minimise any panic. A panic situation in a large crowd could lead to more serious situations arising. Safety is the prime concern of stewards at all times, and as such you must ensure that you follow the correct safety procedures.

Stewards need to be alert for any signs of antisocial or illegal behaviour by spectators, for example, violence or the use of illegal substances. If such situations occur, you must know how and when to intervene. You will need to understand when it is appropriate to deal with problem situations yourself and when you should seek assistance from others.

It is very important that stewards remain alert at all times and aware of what is happening around them, monitoring and identifying any potential crowd problems.

Key terms

Communications resources: these resources could be notebooks for recording incidents, or communications equipment such as radios, if appropriate.

Event: any type of public event (for example a sporting event or musical performance).

Remember: In order to carry out your role as an event steward effectively you need to be:

- well trained
- professional at all times
- impartial
- attentive to individual needs and to the crowd.

Carry out your duties impartially

An important part of the steward's code of conduct is to behave at all times in a professional manner – being polite, courteous and helpful to all spectators regardless of their affiliations. Being **impartial** means that you do not favour anyone when making a decision, acting at all times in good faith and making honest, unbiased decisions with integrity.

We all have certain prejudices and preconceptions, and at times you will have feelings or be slightly biased towards one party or another. For example, it can be difficult not to take sides when two people are arguing, especially when you know someone who is part of the argument. However, it is your job to make sure your personal feelings do not interfere with your professional conduct or get in the way of effective communication.

A **prejudice** is a pre-judgement, i.e., a strong belief, opinion or judgement made without finding out the facts of a case. It is very important not to allow prejudice to influence your decisions when you are working – for example, assuming that all young men who wear hoods are thugs or that all supporters of a particular football team are violent. People will quickly become annoyed if they feel they are being discriminated against or stereotyped, and this type of behaviour from an event steward is unacceptable.

You must follow the venue's procedures, act professionally at all times and offer all customers equal levels of care and respect. If you do not treat people fairly and impartially, this could lead to serious complaints or allegations of illegality.

Identify the basic legal requirements covering disability, discrimination and safety

The main Acts of Parliament covering disability are the Disability Discrimination Acts of 1995, 1999 and 2004. These and other regulations relating to the health and safety of people at events were outlined in Unit 203, pages 10–11. The key areas are that:

- disabled people have a right not to be discriminated against for reasons relating to their disability

- all goods, facilities and services should be accessible and suitable for spectators with disabilities. Reasonable adjustments should be provided, for example, ramps for wheelchairs, access to viewing areas, auxiliary aids, toilet facilities etc.

- health and safety is an issue for all people. Physical barriers should be removed or overcome for people who have particular requirements, except where a person's health and safety might be endangered.

Key terms

Impartial: – not favouring or discriminating against any particular type of person.

Prejudice: – a strong belief, opinion or judgement made without finding out the facts.

What sort of assistance might these customers need?

Key term

Discrimination: the unfair treatment of a person or a group, on the basis of prejudice.

There are two kinds of **discrimination**: direct and indirect. Direct discrimination occurs when people are treated unfairly based on their membership of a particular category or group, for example:

- gender
- sexual orientation
- race
- colour
- nationality
- ethnic or national origin
- age
- employment status
- disability
- language
- religion.

Indirect discrimination occurs when there are rules, regulations or procedures operating, which have the effect of discriminating against certain groups of people. This may happen in subtle ways.

Can you think about how discrimination could take place at a football match? For example:

- a group of supporters in your designated area chants racial abuse at players or opposing fans
- a disabled spectator is unable to gain access to a particular area due to a lack of wheelchair-friendly access
- a group of fans makes sexist remarks to someone of the opposite gender
- an elderly couple are pushed out of the way by a group of rowdy fans.

All of the above examples are examples of discrimination and are illegal. Football clubs across Europe are part of a campaign against racism using footballers as part of the education process in schools, websites, clubs etc. For a link to the website Show Racism The Red Card, please go to www.pearsonhotlinks.co.uk, search for this title and click on the relevant page.

Case study

While **monitoring** my designated area I noticed a family with two small children who were obviously tourists. They were surrounded by a group of about 200 young men gesticulating and chanting loudly. From their body language you could see that they were uncomfortable and concerned.

Over to you

- How would you deal with members of the public who feel intimidated by the surrounding crowd?

- What is your main priority? Is it the need to be impartial to everyone, or to prevent possible conflict and disorder by caring for customers?

Key term

Monitoring: keeping a careful eye on a situation.

Types of crowd

In the course of your duty you will come across all types of crowds. The type of crowd will often depend on the type of event and you will need to adjust your approach accordingly. The study of crowd movement is known as crowd dynamics.

Friendly crowd

You are more likely to have a friendly crowd at family events, for example, a Crufts dog show. You would not expect there to be many problems with a friendly crowd, so if you are dealing with this type of crowd you can be more relaxed and less assertive than you would be with a potentially aggressive crowd. When giving instructions, you should talk to people in a friendly way: ask them to do things rather than giving orders. Be aware that friendly crowds can become excitable and, from there, aggressive. This occasionally happens with football crowds when things start to go wrong.

Aggressive crowd

Highly competitive team sports, for example, a football match or a boxing tournament, are more likely to attract an aggressive crowd. When dealing with this type of crowd, you will need to be more assertive in order to prevent further aggression and possible violence. You should always ask people to do what you require as a first response, but you may have to instruct the crowd if they do not respond. Never shout, as this indicates that you have lost control. Always think clearly and be proactive: you should be constantly carrying out a personal safety risk assessment based on the rapidly changing behaviour of individuals in the

What sort of crowd would you expect at a family event?

Skills builder

When you are working as an event steward you will have plenty of opportunities to talk to all sorts of people.

- Ask one of your colleagues to check your body language, general demeanour and attitude and feed back to you – do you look friendly, professional and approachable?

- Does the way in which you speak to people and deal with them affect your behaviour as well as their attitude to you?

crowd, or of the crowd itself. This is called 'dynamic risk assessment' which we will discuss it in more detail later. What you need to do is keep asking yourself questions based on the information that you are receiving from the crowd:

- ☐ Is the crowd (or individuals within the crowd) simply excited, or is that excitement turning into aggression?

- ☐ Who is the aggression aimed at?

- ☐ Are any of the people in the crowd likely to be injured?

Remember that some people consider abusive language and even threats to be part of an exciting Saturday afternoon out, not a trigger for violence.

Excited crowd

Crowds are likely to get excited at most events. It helps to think of an excited crowd as somewhere between a friendly crowd and an aggressive crowd. Sometimes being excited can cause emotions to boil over, so this type of crowd can turn into an aggressive crowd if it is not monitored carefully. The trick here is to watch out for excited individuals who may start to act in an unsociable way, for example, jostling other people. Some individuals may start to get aggressive with the excited people, and this can lead to a ripple effect where sections of the crowd become aggressive. You need to be assertive in the way that you advise these people, to make sure the situation does not get beyond your control.

Crowd behaviour

In a crowd situation, people's behaviour is likely to be influenced by the behaviour of the people around them. This can be categorised in different ways.

Conformity

If the environment and situation are suitable, people will conform to the behaviour of those around them. People in a crowd will not necessarily behave as they would on their own or in a small group.

Aggression

People may use aggression to create a sense of belonging and solidarity with their own group. For example, spectators at a boxing tournament may let off steam by using aggressive language and behaviour towards one of the boxers and rival supporters.

While such behaviour may appear alarming, it is often no more than ritual behaviour and only rarely turns into actual violence.

Loss of individuality

This is much more than conformity and more like total subsuming of 'self' to the moment – a loss of individual control, swayed by the crowd. For example, a respectable bank manager might invade the pitch at a football match and later be unable to explain why.

Venue areas

Confined areas

Every venue will have at least one confined area, for example:

☐ refreshment areas

☐ bars

☐ toilets.

Problems can arise when everyone is trying to get to a confined area at the same time, for example, when the audience rushes to the bar or toilets together during a break. The mass movement of people can lead to crushing, jostling, and sometimes aggressive behaviour or injury due to overcrowding. Too many people being in one area at the same time can also cause some people to feel distress, including claustrophobia and disorientation, with people (including children) getting separated from the main group.

Open areas

Some events will take place in open areas, for example:

☐ outdoor music events

☐ exhibition venues

☐ fairs in parks or fields.

There will also be open areas at most venues, such as entrance halls, the main arena, etc.

Open areas have no structure, which can cause its own problems. For example, there might be several different types of crowd moving around freely and interacting with each other. In an open area, people standing or sitting may obstruct the movement of the crowd. There might also be crowds coming in from different directions. If they meet in the middle, or their passage is blocked and they are not controlled properly, this can lead to problems with crowd density, which can lead to injury and, in the worst cases, death.

Weather conditions can also have an impact on crowd behaviour. For example, sudden heavy rain, thunder or lightning can cause people to run for cover and whole sections of crowd might head for the same area. This can lead to aggressive behaviour as people strive to reach shelter first. There could already be people in the sheltered area who will probably be unprepared for the sudden increase in crowd density. This can result in people being trampled, especially if it is muddy. In this way, a friendly crowd can easily become an excited crowd as a result of an unexpected incident. They are then more likely to develop into an aggressive crowd.

Public areas

Lots of events take place in public areas, like streets or town centres, for example:

- street parades
- royal visits
- marathons, cycling events
- continental markets
- surf festivals
- maritime events
- celebrity funerals
- carnivals, fairs.

What sort of issues would you watch out for at this event?

Although some events that take place in public areas will be ticketed, a lot are unticketed, which means you will have no idea how many people to expect. Unanticipated large crowds can completely change the actions that have been planned to control the situation.

At certain events, such as a street carnival where the procession moves through the streets in convoy on motor vehicles, there are likely to be lots of people standing on the pavement spectating. You may need to watch out for:

- overcrowding on the pavement
- jostling, which can lead to people being forced into the path of an oncoming vehicle
- spectators being argumentative and potentially aggressive due to being pushed or jostled
- children running into the street
- drunken spectators (a danger to themselves and others)
- damage to buildings or scaffolding as a result of people climbing to get a better view
- rubbish in the street or rubbish bins which are **hazards** and provide possible missiles to throw at people/procession.

Non-public areas

Some events are held in non-public, or private, areas such as:

- the VIP lounge at a venue
- private clubs
- back stage parties
- corporate hospitality events
- private dinner parties
- weddings
- children's parties at venues.

The venue where you are employed as an event steward may also require your professional approach at any number of private events that occur during the course of a year. Many guests will arrive and produce an invitation to the party. Invitations are similar to tickets and therefore guests will need to be treated in the same way as people who have tickets: they need to be verified as genuine guests before being allowed in.

Identify crowd problems

It is your responsibility as a steward to pay close attention to the crowd in your designated area, and monitor it carefully to prevent minor disturbances building

Key term

Hazard: anything with the potential to cause harm (e.g. electricity, hazardous substances, excessive noise).

Functional skills

English: Reading – Stewards need to be able to read the information on an invitation and verify that the person is in possession of a genuine invitation.

Unit 206

Monitor spectators and deal with crowd problems

into major crowd problems. You should report any potential or actual crowd problems to your supervisor or control room as they arise. Table 206.1 shows some typical crowd problems.

At some events, there will be a control room, which will use CCTV equipment to monitor a venue. There may also be people with binoculars to identify potential problems. However, you are the 'eyes and ears' on the ground and should remain vigilant.

What you are looking for when monitoring a crowd can be divided into three main sections — the three 'D's.

- **Density** — the number of spectators walking, sitting or standing together in an area. The more people in the area, the denser the crowd. Overcrowding can cause real issues. A number of scientific studies have been carried out into the effects of crowd density on the behaviour of individuals, as well as on crowd dynamics.

- **Dynamics** — again the subject of a great deal of research over the years. Dynamics in its simplest form is about the patterns of crowd actions, the movement of spectators (often led by individuals) and the heightened emotions that influence collective behaviour. Sudden or unexpected movements within a crowd can cause real problems.

- **Distress** — this can relate to individuals, to just a part of the crowd or to the whole. Crowds can become anxious due to density, dynamics or other influences such as the event performance, weather conditions, exhaustion, physical discomfort or the behaviour of individuals or crowds in other areas.

Type of crowd problem	Signs of the problem	Possible action
Sudden and unexpected crowd movement	<ul><li>standing in a seated area</li><li>surging</li><li>swaying, including sideways, forwards or backwards</li><li>crowd surfing.</li></ul>	Monitor carefully and inform supervisor
Local overcrowding – too many people in one section of the venue	<ul><li>rushing to get to a part of the venue</li><li>crowding at break time to use facilities</li><li>pushing and shoving to create room</li><li>signs of frustration and people getting angry.</li></ul> If only the heads of the spectators can be seen, the maximum density of the enclosure or section may have been exceeded. This can lead to pressure within the crowd making it very difficult for individuals or groups to control their own movement. This in turn can quickly lead to distress, anxiety and aggression.	Monitor carefully, carry out a dynamic risk assessment, inform supervisor

Table 206.1 Typical crowd problems and possible actions

Table 206.1 Typical crowd problems and possible actions (cont.)

Type of crowd problem	Signs of the problem	Possible action
Over-capacity – too many people in the venue overall	The capacity of a venue must be strictly controlled and managed and must not be exceeded for safety reasons. Calculations have to be made relating to the entry of people, the holding capacity, the exit capacity and the emergency evacuation capacity; all of these numbers have to be provided for each venue/event and are part of the risk assessment.	Monitor carefully and inform supervisor
Distress, including claustrophobia, disorientation, fatigue, vertigo	• facial expressions • language • signs • ignoring instructions and trying to get out of the way. Distress needs to be recognised as soon as possible and dealt with quickly. Distress can lead to serious injury, suffering and pain.	Monitor carefully, inform supervisor, remain calm and customer-focused
Separation of individuals and groups	Shock, distress, wandering or rushing around; individuals may be in tears, confused, upset, concerned and demanding. Creates distress and trauma especially for vulnerable people who have particular needs, such as: • people with language and/or cultural differences • people with disabilities • children or older people.	Inform supervisor and colleagues, remain calm and customer-focused
Unsocial behaviour (often associated with consuming too much alcohol)	• swearing • urinating in public • unnecessary noise or nuisance. Some people are likely to be offended by such behaviour (depending on the event and the crowd type).	Inform supervisor, assess situation and observe behaviour
Unlawful behaviour	• public disorder • racist chanting • drunkenness • throwing objects • threatening behaviour • breach of the peace • assault or serious assault • theft, robbery, forgery (usually of tickets) • football offences (e.g. throwing objects onto the pitch, indecent or racist chanting, entry into restricted areas, being drunk inside the ground, possession of alcohol or container)	Inform supervisor, observe behaviour
Entry into restricted areas	Avoiding communication and contact with others while trying to obtain entry. Restricted areas may be due to: • a health and safety risk in that area • the need to keep visiting fans separate from home fans due to the risk of violence • the area is already at capacity level • the area may be designated for VIPs or performers • equipment or vehicles may be operating in that area.	Inform supervisor, observe and monitor

How would you deal with someone who is trying to gain access to a restricted area?

Other causes of problems within the venue, which could impact on crowd behaviour, include:

- power cuts
- late arrivals or delays in starting event
- gas or chemical leaks
- structural damage
- weather conditions
- suspected terrorist incidents such as a suspect package or bomb threat.

Best Practice Checklist

Helping people with problems

- Try to get used to thinking proactively – look for the signs of potential problems and deal with them before they happen.
- Remain alert at all times and aware of what is happening around you.
- Make sure you are professional, polite, courteous and calm at all times.
- All decisions must be made impartially, without favour to anyone.
- Be aware of the different types of crowds and learn to adjust your approach accordingly.
- Know which areas the public are allowed into and the restricted areas.
- Know what you are looking for when monitoring crowds – remember the three 'D's.

Follow instructions and procedures to deal with crowd problems

Assess and report crowd problems

When you are monitoring a crowd, you are looking at the behaviour of the crowd and carrying out **assessments**, making a decision as to whether a problem or incident needs to be dealt with immediately, or deferred, or not dealt with at all. The decision you make will depend on how much information you and others have. For example, the control room may be receiving reports from others who are viewing a potential problem from a different angle, or pictures from cameras at the venue. You may receive information and questions relating to what you can see from your position on the ground and you must communicate clearly and accurately, whether via a radio or face to face. Say what you can see and hear and then follow any instructions given to you.

 Remember: You are not on your own; you are part of a team with a supervisor and you are all working together, communicating and watching each other, as well as the crowd.

As mentioned before, when monitoring any crowd, think about the three 'D's — the crowd's:

- ☐ dynamics
- ☐ density
- ☐ distress.

Be vigilant: keep an eye out for any changes in the crowd

Key term

Assess: gather all necessary information relating to a crowd problem and work out the level of risk to yourself and others.

Remember: Adhering to procedures correctly is important in any disciplined and managed organisation.

As you observe the crowd you are assessing what could happen and the severity of any injury that may occur. In other words:

☐ Is something going to happen?

☐ If something does happen, how serious is it likely to be?

☐ Could people get hurt, and if so, how serious could the injuries be?

An event steward should be constantly evaluating this risk and then reporting back to a supervisor.

When you are monitoring a crowd you need to ask yourself: 'What will be the consequences of my decision?' If the decision is to eject the person from the venue, could this actually create more problems and escalate the risk? It may be difficult to remove someone who is struggling from a seated area, getting other people to move, or negotiating stairways, and the spectator's behaviour may be the same as that of others, part of a ritual that occurs every week. What will their reaction be, how will the opposing spectators react?

To make a decision, you need to be in possession of all the facts and to talk to your supervisor about the options available before making a decision. The final decision will probably be made by others such as your line manager or supervisor, and will always be based on the likelihood of injury to anyone involved.

Think about it

What are the procedures at your venue if you observe a potential crowd problem?

- Write down what you think could happen if you said nothing and kept observing a potential problem.
- What might happen if you tried to deal with the problem yourself?
- Ask to see a risk assessment about the risk of crowd behaviour.

Reporting should always be carried out using the correct 'chain of command'. For a steward, the next person in the chain of command is your supervisor, whether the report is given orally (face to face or via radio or telephone) or in writing.

Remember that all reports need to be accurate and concise. You could be called into court as a witness to an incident, so you need to make sure you know all the facts. All reports, whether in your notebook or on official paper, must be completed as soon as possible after the incident, as the court will want to know exactly when and where the report was completed. The longer the period between the incident happening and the report being completed, the less chance there is of the report being accurate.

You must always follow organisational procedures. No two incidents are the same and they will all need to be managed and reported according to the situation; however, the basic principles give you a starting point.

Though most of your reports will be oral, occasionally you may have to complete an incident or accident report. Figure 206.1 shows a typical incident report form detailing an accident that was dealt with by an event steward.

Incident or Accident report form		
REPORTING PERSON *Una Croft*	TIME *15:00*	DATE *22 March 2011*
LOCATION OF INCIDENT *Outside the front door of Mary's Toy Shop, Corner of James Avenue and Henry Street, Williamstown.*		
DESCRIPTION OF INCIDENT OR ACCIDENT *At 14:55 on Tuesday 22 March 2011, Mr Julian Hodges was standing on top of a chair in the entrance of Mary's Toy Shop at the address above watching the annual procession pass by in Henry Street. At the time of the incident, James Avenue and Henry Street were full of spectators watching the procession. As the first float approached the junction of James Avenue and Henry Street, the crowd of spectators surged forward, knocking the chair and Mr Hodges fell off the chair onto his arm, injuring himself. I informed my supervisor, Lizzie Lockett, who summoned a first aider. Mr Hodges was later taken to hospital with a suspected broken elbow.* Signed: *U. F. Croft* Date: *22/3/2011*		
DIAGRAM OF INCIDENT LOCATION Draw a diagram here WHEN COMPLETED HAND TO YOUR LINE MANAGER		
LINE MANAGER FOR COMMENT/ACTION		
NAME OF LINE MANAGER		
DEPARTMENT/AREA		
SIGNATURE:		DATE:

Figure 206.1 An example of an incident report form

Functional skills

English: Writing – writing a report will allow you to practise your writing skills.

Best Practice Checklist

Practise writing an incident report. Make sure that it is accurate, stating clearly:

☐ **Who** is writing the report?

☐ **Who** was involved in the incident?

☐ **When** it happened

☐ **Where** it happened

☐ **What** happened?

☐ **How** it happened

☐ **Why** it happened.

The five 'Ws' (and one H)
I keep six honest serving-men
(They taught me all I knew)
Their names are What and Why and When
And How and Where and Who.

Rudyard Kipling, *Just So Stories*

Being proactive is a really important part of the role of a steward. The more you become aware of potential problems and do something about them before issues happen, the less likelihood there will be of an incident occurring.

During the last learning outcome we discussed the type of crowd problems that might occur. It is vital that you take prompt action if you see problems occurring.

 Remember: Risks are not static – they may escalate or de-escalate rapidly in response to individual or crowd behaviour. You will need to assess the changing risks continually – this is known as dynamic risk assessment.

Take action following instructions and agreed procedures

There are many types of crowd problem and the procedures to follow in each case will be agreed and written down. These will outline what actions you should take, which should be taken as soon as possible after the problem has been identified. An early response to an actual or potential problem should always be to:

☐ remain alert, calm and professional – remember, your behaviour and attitude will affect the people around you

☐ report the problem immediately and clearly to your supervisor/control room

☐ ask for help to deal with the problem

- maintain your own personal safety as well as the safety of the public and your colleagues

- focus on your roles and responsibilities, remaining customer-centred

- remain visible to the crowd and continue to update everyone involved as the situation changes.

In general, the people at an event are there to enjoy themselves; if you follow the procedure outlined above as soon as you spot a potential problem, you should be able to prevent the situation from becoming unmanageable. However, if this does not work, you will need to follow the instructions from your supervisor or control room and take action such as:

- reassuring or warning individuals or groups

- requesting the removal or ejection of people or objects

- containing the crowd to ensure that problems are not repeated.

You must always assess the possible risks before you take any action and you must follow the venue's policies and procedures. Think quickly but carefully about your actions and consider the potential dangers to yourself and others – personal safety and the safety of your colleagues and the people in your area are paramount.

Asking your colleagues for support could help you to deal with a situation before it gets out of hand

Skills builder

In the venue where you are working, there will be a risk assessment which has been written for the above locations and covers your personal safety.

- Ask if you can see a risk assessment form and identify one of more of the personal safety risks which relate to these locations.

- Ask if you can help to complete a risk assessment form for your designated area.

Think about it

In your designated area, what do you think might involve a potential personal safety problem? Write down a list of potential personal safety hazards that could occur in the following locations:

- car park
- bar or beer tent
- queue
- staircases and **vomitories**.

Key term

Vomitory: an entrance or exit at any level of a stadium, leading to the seating areas and providing access to other parts of the stadium.

Communicate with the people involved and colleagues clearly

Communicating with people is always a priority as this will provide everyone involved — including your colleagues — with information. Accurate and clear information provides the background to the support or resources needed for dealing with an incident. Your attitude and behaviour must be professional.

Clear and assertive communication is also required when dealing with an incident; people need to know exactly what is expected of them and what will happen in the event of non-compliance. The key is to establish order, get people's attention as quickly as possible and avoid an escalation of the problem. On these occasions people are looking for a leader able to offer a solution to the problem.

Reassure people and encourage calm behaviour

We discussed earlier the need to remain calm at all times and the ways in which a steward's attitude and behaviour will rub off on other people. Remember it is absolutely vital to avoid panic in an emergency situation.

- Your attitude and behaviour will have a big effect on the spectators and your colleagues. Do not panic! Remain calm, reassure the people around you, and be assertive; make sure you match your words, tone and body language.

- Act professionally in directing people towards the course of action required.

In an incident your uniform will identify you as someone to turn to, and it is vital that you appear well trained, knowledgeable, professional and capable of dealing with the situation. If you are unable to react effectively in an emergency, people will panic, endangering you and others around you.

Case study

I am an experienced event steward used to different types of crowds, and over the years I have seen the many ways in which they react to events.

Before I go out to work in the morning I think about my attitude and how it is likely to affect my behaviour. I know my attitude changes daily depending on what has happened in my personal life and how I feel generally. I even stand in front of the mirror after I have put my uniform on and think, 'How approachable do I look today?'

Over to you

- How do you think you look to other people? For example, do you appear approachable, friendly and helpful?

- How would you check to make sure you have the right attitude and behaviour before you meet the public?

Describe basic conflict management techniques and defensive tactics

Earlier in this unit we discussed how you will need to remain visible to the crowd, reassuring people and on some occasions warning them, and as a last resort removing people and objects.

We have also spoken about the need to carry out 'dynamic risk assessments'. This is when you have to make decisions on the spot about risks as they present themselves, deciding on the appropriate response and monitoring any further developments as a result of decisions being made.

Basic conflict management techniques apply the same principles. You are visible as a person who has authority and responsibility and your communication skills are important. You need to remain customer-focused, supportive and friendly (but assertive when required) – remember that your attitude and behaviour will influence the people around you. When someone becomes argumentative or shows signs of aggression you need all of these skills as well as the ability to carry out dynamic risk assessments, monitor whether your attempts at defusing the situation are working or whether the signs of aggression are rising.

Remember: the best defensive tactic is to remove yourself from danger. If this is not possible, ensure you have an escape route and never put yourself at risk in any conflict situation. Work with your colleagues and request assistance if there is any chance you will need it. Conflict management is covered in greater detail in Unit 201, Help to manage conflict, page 85.

 Remember: Don't forget that your attitude can subconsciously influence someone else's attitude and behaviour and may escalate potential conflict. This is a skill and will need to be practised carefully. Next time you go to work think about your attitude, about how you look and how you will come across to other people.

Keep the control room/supervisor informed

The control room and the staff in it are a valuable resource and a vital part of your team. The control room is the hub of all information and intelligence being received before, during and after the event. Keeping the control room fully informed of any potential situation (e.g. hazards and risks, crowd problems etc.) is therefore very important.

Information received at an early stage could allow you to de-escalate a situation before it develops into a full-blown crowd management problem or **emergency**.

Your information could also be used to prevent an incident from occurring, by informing others such as the emergency services, local authority, your colleagues or the public.

Key term

Emergency: any situation that immediately threatens the health and safety of spectators, staff or yourself, for example fires, bomb threats.

Remember:

- Failure in communications will lead to poor incident management.
- If you do not communicate and respond as required, you may be a significant hazard to public safety.

The control room is the hub of all information

As well as monitoring the crowd dynamics in your designated area and reporting any problems as soon as they occur, you need to establish a rapport with the spectators and your colleagues. If you talk to people as they arrive — letting them know why you are there and what the rules are — you may help prevent a major incident.

 Remember: You are the customer-facing representative, talking to spectators, remaining professional, alert, reliable and customer-focused.

Best Practice Checklist ✓

- ☐ Get used to watching the crowd carefully in your designated area.

- ☐ Report any potential problems that you see immediately.

- ☐ Practise sending clear, accurate messages.

- ☐ Actively listen to any instructions that you receive and follow them.

- ☐ At all times try to keep calm, alert and professional.

- ☐ Always assess the risk before you take any action; the personal safety of yourself and your colleagues is also very important.

- ☐ Keep everyone informed of the situation and reassure the people who you are dealing with.

Talk to spectators as often as you can – this could help you prevent an incident

Working Life

Indira's story

This year I was an event steward at a big carnival in my town. A full risk assessment was prepared by the company, the emergency services and the council, and procedures were agreed. At the pre-event briefing they gave us resources and information about the event.

A carnival is full of potential dangers to vulnerable people. We were warned that in previous years people had tried to climb onto scaffolding, shop and bus stop canopies, and even onto buildings and the roofs of vehicles. At carnivals spectators also tend to arrive late and push their way in front of people who have waited for hours, or walk on the road. Last year this caused annoyance among the crowd and a number of spectators became violent.

When I took my position, I did a quick assessment and reported some concerns to my supervisor about the number of people standing on a busy junction. There were babies in push chairs near the front, and I was worried about the safety of youngsters and elderly people if the crowd started pushing. We redistributed the crowd slowly and calmly, relieving pressure on the front and avoiding a potentially distressing situation.

Ask the expert

Q **What should I do if I see someone committing a criminal offence, such as assaulting someone?**

A Let your supervisor, control room and colleagues know immediately. Ask for help, and provide a full account of what is happening. Qualified people will help you straight away.

Q **What would I do if I saw a young child walk into a dangerous area, for example, into the path of a lorry taking part in a street procession?**

A Stop the procession immediately and remove the child to a safe place; inform your supervisor/control room; recommence the procession and deal with the incident as a lost child.

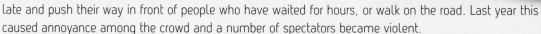

Top tips

✓ When you arrive at your designated area, carry out a risk assessment. You will need to keep re-assessing the risk as time and circumstances change.

✓ When you communicate to your supervisor or the control room, be as accurate, clear and factual as possible. Report what you can see and hear.

✓ Remain customer-focused at all times.

Check your knowledge

1. Explain why it is important to carefully observe crowds and areas.

2. Describe what to look for when you monitor a crowd.

3. Why is it important to carry out your duties impartially?

4. What type of hazards might you find in these areas?
   - confined areas
   - open areas
   - public areas.

5. Describe the sort of personal conduct and appearance that you should aspire to.

6. Describe the procedures to follow for each type of crowd problem.

7. Explain why it is important to reassure the people involved and encourage them to be calm during an incident or an emergency.

8. Identify the types of action which might lead to stewards endangering themselves and others.

9. Describe how to assess the seriousness of a problem.

10. Explain why it's important to communicate clearly with the people involved and with colleagues.

Getting ready for assessment

Once you have had some experience of, and feel confident in monitoring crowds and identifying potential problems, and have followed instructions as well as procedures to deal with crowd problems, you will be ready to be assessed towards this unit.

You will have to prove that you have the correct resources at all times, and that you have been involved in dealing with different types of crowds and crowd problems in different areas of a venue.

You will also need to show that you have dealt with different types of people and know how to carry out actions correctly.

Unit 201

Help to manage conflict

This unit is about recognising and responding to potential or actual situations where there is, or is likely to be, conflict occurring between people. The unit includes carrying out personal risk assessments, using effective communication (verbal and non-verbal), identifying body language signs and signals, using techniques to defuse the situation, maintaining your own personal safety, giving advice and warnings, and calling for assistance when required. In this unit you will learn how to be aware of your own personal safety while at work, how and when to take appropriate action, how to intervene at the right time and how to seek assistance from others who you work with.

The unit does not include attempting to physically control or restrain people.

You will learn how to:

☐ communicate with people in conflict situations
☐ follow procedures to resolve conflict.

Communicate with people in conflict situations

Communication is not just about talking to people; it is about active listening and providing a positive professional image by using the right body language and non-verbal signals.

The importance of effective communication with people in conflict situations and how poor communication can make situations worse

Communicating with people is a life skill; common sense will tell you that a good communicator is good at developing relationships, as well as someone you feel you can trust. The opposite of a good communicator is a person who finds it difficult to build relationships and trust. This is because we often fail to respond to what is perceived as negative feelings or body language.

Good communication skills are your biggest strength. You will need to **communicate** with people at all times – before the event starts, at break times and as they are leaving.

Good communication is also a key part of customer service and allows you to keep people provided with information and advice. More importantly, it will allow you to recognise and deal with potential **conflict** in a way that minimises risks to yourself and others.

An effective technique in customer care is to ask a person, 'Can I help you?' This will often start a conversation and focus attention on you. At the same time, if you use the right body language, showing the other person that you mean no harm and that you are there to help with any problem, you will be breaking down barriers and creating an opportunity to talk. This is known as signalling non-aggression.

It is important to ensure that your communications are clear and not open to misinterpretation. People are likely to hear what they want to hear, and if this is not what you intended it will be more difficult for you to maintain control. Figure 201.1 shows an example of a simple misunderstanding which could have potentially deadly consequences!

If anything is unclear, it is your responsibility to ask questions until you are sure you understand the situation fully.

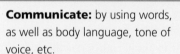

Key terms

Communicate: by using words, as well as body language, tone of voice, etc.

Conflict: situations in which people disagree strongly, which may lead to violence or other forms of unlawful or unsociable behaviour.

Functional skills

English: Speaking, listening and communication – these skills show that you can obtain information from people, explain things clearly and reduce the risk of disagreement.

You should also be aware that there are many 'blocks to communication' – things that may hinder or prevent communication. Possible blocks include:

- ☐ noise from speakers or people talking, shouting or singing
- ☐ physical discomfort (crowd density, temperature, tiredness, hunger)
- ☐ people's moods and emotional state
- ☐ people's attitudes and values
- ☐ alcohol or drug use
- ☐ cultural or language differences
- ☐ mental health problems.

Think about it

Think about the volume of your voice. Are you shouting because it's loud in the stadium, because you want to get your point across, because you are beginning to get annoyed, or because you are responding to the tone and volume of the customer's voice?

'I've lost my cat! She's got black fur and very sharp claws.'

'Yes sir. Black fur, claws....'

Figure 201:1 Simple misunderstandings can have potentially deadly consequences!

As an event steward, perhaps the most frequent blocks you encounter will be noise and alcohol. Alcohol affects people's ability to react quickly and to understand what is being said to them. It can also affect their attitude, behaviour and predictability, so if you are communicating with someone whom you suspect has been consuming alcohol you should:

- remain calm and speak slowly
- repeat information or requests if necessary
- watch your body language and take care not to look aggressive
- keep a safe distance from the person.
- Explain your actions or requests and ensure your meaning is clear – get **feedback** from the people around you.
- Be assertive, but do not shout.
- If someone is behaving badly, tell them that their behaviour is unacceptable but avoid talking down to them or criticising their actions.
- Be respectful and maintain a professional approach at all times.

> **Key term**
>
> **Feedback:** comments from other people (customers or colleagues), telling you what they think.

Using body language and other non-verbal types of communication

There are a number of different ways in which people receive communication, mainly using the senses of hearing and sight. When we speak to people the message is communicated through our:

- words
- tone of voice – the way in which we deliver our words
- non-verbal communication – the way we stand, our expressions and the gestures we use.

Research shows that the strongest message that a person receives from you is likely to be from non-verbal communication (body language).

Communication	Meaning and understanding received
Words	7%
Tone of voice	38%
Non-verbal	55%

Table 201.1 How different methods of communicating are received

Words alone do not make much impact on the person that you are communicating with, unless you match your tone and non-verbal communication to your words. When you first meet a customer, your attitude should be pleasant, welcoming and helpful. If you greet someone with a smile, they will usually respond by smiling back. On the other hand, if you are moody or aggressive, the customer is likely to mirror your attitude and react in the same way.

The important signals that you need to provide are related to the following factors.

Posture

- Folding your arms will send out a negative signal, such as, 'I don't want to talk to you', 'I'm not going to listen' or 'I've made my mind up'.
- Standing with your hands on your hips will make you look unwelcoming.
- A relaxed posture will make others feel at ease.
- Showing the palms of your hands is a good non-threatening gesture. (This was used historically to show that you were not carrying a weapon.)
- Looking upwards or raising your eyebrows when you are listening or talking to someone is a sign that you are getting impatient or irritated by the other person.
- Looking down or lowering your eyes can make people feel inferior.
- Unfriendly facial expressions (such as a frown) imply you do not want to talk to others.

Position

Remember that where you are positioned relates to the type of relationship that you have with someone and where you want to be to maintain a safe space. Your personal risk assessment will need to take account of exit routes, both for you and the other person. Never put yourself into a corner that you can't escape from, and never block anyone in — always allow people the opportunity to walk away, so they don't have to try to fight their way out of a corner.

Try to control your body language, as other people will react to it

Movements

☐ Finger pointing, or jabbing movements with a finger, is aggressive and can signal that you are arguing with someone. It can also cause the other person to be embarrassed, which may create further conflict.

☐ Keep all movements deliberate and slow. You do not want to unnerve the customer with fast arm movements which might give out the wrong signals.

Hand gestures

Hands are a very important part of the non-verbal communication process:

☐ Showing your upturned palms is a recognised signal of non-aggression.

☐ Keeping your hands behind your back can be confusing (the person may think you are hiding something) and is unsafe practice, leaving your body totally open.

☐ Clenching your fists, even with your arms at your side, is a sign of aggression and tension.

Remember: Remember what we said about good communication skills.

● Your body language and tone of voice are very important.

● Empathy is a very strong tool for a communicator: it breaks down barriers.

● 'It's not what you say, it's the way that you say it, and that's what gets results.'

Best Practice Checklist

Managing your tone of voice

☐ Speak clearly and calmly without raising your voice. People will understand what you are saying and be more likely to accept it as fact.

☐ Never shout at anyone. If you need to be more assertive, raise your voice, but always remain customer-focused and professional.

☐ Never argue or talk down to anyone.

Managing your body language

☐ Actively listen and empathise to show that you understand the person's feelings.

☐ Non-verbal signs will show that you are listening and understand.

☐ Be aware of your posture, movements and hand gestures.

Skills builder

You are an experienced steward and have been asked to supervise three new stewards as they meet and greet customers entering the venue.

During the afternoon you talk to the event stewards about the importance of body language and ask whether they can recognise signs of possible conflict from the following body language:

- **Frowning:** What will people think if you look annoyed, unsociable or depressed? How will your attitude affect that of other people?

- **Looking down on people:** How do you feel when someone looks down on you? Practise lowering your head, rather than your eyes; lowering your eyes has the effect of looking down on someone and can make them feel unimportant.

- **Finger pointing:** Finger pointing can look aggressive and is personal. If you point your finger at someone, you are invading their space and showing aggression.

- **Hands on hips:** Putting your hands on your hips can make you look superior and hostile. Always keep your hands and arms relaxed and by your side.

- **Folding your arms:** This makes you appear distrustful and can signal that you are not willing to listen to the other person.

- **Sudden movement:** This can easily be misinterpreted as a sign of imminent attack.

- **Rolling your eyes upwards:** This is usually a sign of frustration and annoyance.

Body language plays an important part in communication. What does this steward's body language tell you?

Follow procedures to resolve conflict

In previous units we have discussed the need to follow your organisation's procedures at all times. You will be told about any relevant procedures during the pre-event briefing. These procedures will outline how you should monitor and observe individuals or groups and deal with a variety of circumstances (e.g. minor complaints which could escalate or more obvious issues). At any event, in any venue, there are likely to be 'hotspots', triggers or special circumstances where aggression or conflict could occur.

Conflict occurs for a number of reasons, some directly connected to the event or circumstances surrounding it, and others that the customer brings with them, for example, personal issues that affect their attitude and behaviour on that day or at that moment.

Your personal safety has to be the number one priority, especially in conflict situations. Unless you look after yourself and carry out risk assessments before putting yourself or others into any situation, you may be endangering yourself and other people.

Dynamic risk assessment

Dynamic risk assessment can be defined as a continuous assessment of risk — and appropriate measures to reduce this risk — in a rapidly changing situation. As a personal safety situation develops, you need to be constantly asking yourself questions about how the level of risk is changing.

The majority of potential conflict situations can be prevented if seen and identified at an early stage. This requires customer care skills, a professional approach and a good knowledge of your role as an event steward. For example, customers kept waiting in a queue for a long time will become frustrated and annoyed, so you need to provide them with information (about the reasons for the delay, waiting times etc.) and do what you can to make them comfortable. This will create a good impression and should help to prevent any conflict from occurring.

Think about it

Think about the cycle of attitude and behaviour and the way in which a person's attitude can affect the behaviour of others and therefore increase or reduce the likelihood of conflict. Can you examine your attitude on the way to an event and think about it? Are you happy, sad, in a bad or good mood? How will this affect your behaviour and therefore the attitude and behaviour of people you are dealing with at the event?

Is there anything you can do to consciously change your attitude? Attitudes are very difficult to change, but if you recognise your own negative feelings and put these out of sight when dealing with people, you will be able to control your behaviour and reduce the likelihood of conflict.

Types of conflict situation and the correct responses

Conflict situations can occur for all sorts of reasons, some of which are not directly connected to the event, the venue, the management, or you. People sometimes carry conflict with them and an opportunity arises for the conflict to occur. An argument or disagreement that happened earlier in the day for instance, and which has not been resolved, can sometimes re-appear for the smallest of reasons.

The main types of conflict situation at events are:

☐ aggressive behaviour (e.g. shouting, shaking fists, spitting)

☐ aggressive language (e.g. swearing, threatening to assault other people)

☐ personal abuse

☐ racial abuse and chanting

☐ sudden and unexpected anger or frustration between people

☐ assault.

How would you deal with people in a queue who are visibly getting annoyed?

Think about it

Read through the list below. In which locations or circumstances are you most likely to encounter challenging behaviour from people at an event?

- People have to queue for long periods of time
- People have been drinking too much alcohol
- People have come to the venue with the wrong attitude
- Someone is refused entry
- Someone is stopped and searched
- Someone refuses to be searched
- Someone is attempting to enter without a ticket
- Someone is in possession of a forged ticket
- People are carrying prohibited items
- Someone is subject to a banning order for the venue
- People in confined areas are being pushed and shoved by people in the crowd
- Someone is detained for committing an illegal act such as:
  - drinking alcohol at a football stadium
  - throwing missiles
  - entering a prohibited or unauthorised area
  - using abusive, racist or indecent language
  - persistently standing in a seated area.

Case study

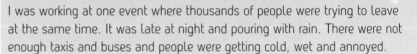

I was working at one event where thousands of people were trying to leave at the same time. It was late at night and pouring with rain. There were not enough taxis and buses and people were getting cold, wet and annoyed.

I saw a young man being pushed from behind by a number of people due to sudden crowd movement as a bus appeared. The man started to act unreasonably and a full-blown argument with another person broke out, which was totally out of proportion to the incident.

Over to you

- What do you think you should do to prevent conflict?
- What do you think could have been done at the planning stage to reduce the chances of this occurring?

Table 201.2 shows some possible responses to the situations listed above.

Conflict situation	Considered response
Aggressive behaviour and abuse to others	Personal risk assessment
	Dynamic risk assessment
	Do nothing other than observe and monitor
	Communication and reasoning
	Provide advice or warning
	Consider ejection
	Conflict management techniques
	If behaviour continues seek assistance
Aggressive language and threats to others	Personal risk assessment
	Dynamic risk assessment
	Do nothing other than observe and monitor
	Communication and reasoning
	Provide advice or warning
	Consider ejection
	Conflict management techniques including de-escalation and diffusion
	If behaviour continues seek assistance
Personal abuse	Personal risk assessment
	Dynamic risk assessment
	Additional care required if abuse has turned to you personally
	Seek assistance immediately and continue communication and reasoning
	Provide advice or warning
	Consider ejection
	Conflict management techniques including de-escalation and diffusion
Racial abuse and chanting	Personal risk assessment
	Dynamic risk assessment
	Communication and reasoning
	Provide advice or warning
	Consider ejection/arrest
	Conflict management techniques
	If behaviour continues seek assistance

Table 201.2 Types of conflict situation and possible responses

Table 201.2 Types of conflict situation and possible responses (cont.)

Conflict situation	Considered response
Sudden anger and frustration	Personal risk assessment
	Dynamic risk assessment
	Communication and reasoning
	Provide advice or warning
	Conflict management techniques including de-escalation and diffusion
	If behaviour continues seek assistance
Assault	Personal risk assessment
	Dynamic risk assessment
	Seek assistance immediately
	SIA licensed staff or police may detain and may use force if necessary to physically restrain, eject/arrest

The organisation that you are employed by and the venue will explain carefully what they expect you to do and how to deal with challenging behaviour. It is their responsibility (under the Health and Safety at Work Act) to make sure that you are aware of and comply with company policy at all times.

In Unit 205, pages 48–50 we discussed the limitations of an event steward's role compared with someone who is licensed under the Security Industry Act (an SIA-licensed door supervisor for example). SIA-licensed door supervisors will be trained to deal with conflict and will know how to detain and eject people; many are also trained in physical restraint and disengagement skills. In contrast, your role as an event steward is very straightforward: you should observe, communicate and report to your supervisor or control room.

The organisation's procedure should explain clearly what is expected of you. The venue will expect you to:

☐ be polite, courteous and professional at all times

☐ deal with the public (including complaints or signs of conflict) in a controlled way

☐ defuse aggression

☐ create solutions to problems.

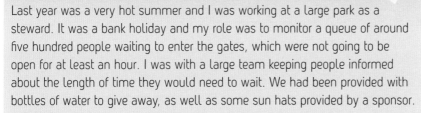

Case study

Last year was a very hot summer and I was working at a large park as a steward. It was a bank holiday and my role was to monitor a queue of around five hundred people waiting to enter the gates, which were not going to be open for at least an hour. I was with a large team keeping people informed about the length of time they would need to wait. We had been provided with bottles of water to give away, as well as some sun hats provided by a sponsor.

A member of the public started complaining that his feet hurt and wanted to go inside so he could sit down. He said he would never come again unless I did something. Other people were getting fed up with him, and one said that if I didn't do something they would deal with him themselves. I offered bottles of water and sun hats, but the first man threw his on the ground and came towards me shouting.

Over to you

☐ What do you think the best plan of action would be under these circumstances?

☐ Do you consider that you have treated everyone fairly?

☐ Have you shown empathy and consideration?

☐ Have you communicated in a way that is likely to defuse conflict?

☐ Were you able to finish with a 'win–win' situation?

Maintain personal space

Maintaining **personal space** is a key part of any personal risk assessment and will help you to stay in control of conflict. Other people may try to get closer to you and invade your personal space so you will need to practise moving around, or stepping backwards or sideways at the right time, to maintain your personal space.

Respect the personal space of others

We all have four personal space 'zones', also known as 'social distances' or 'body space'. These affect how comfortable we feel around other people when they are in those 'zones', and how other people feel when we are in their space. It is important to understand how personal space and feelings of discomfort can affect behaviour.

Key term

Personal space: the amount of space a person needs around them in order to feel comfortable. Getting too close to someone – invading their personal space – is likely to make a difficult situation worse.

The four zones are difficult to measure accurately, because we are all different and they can be affected by our moods or attitudes. However, the general rule is that:

☐ *intimate space* is reserved for close relatives and friends. It is usually by invitation only and an invasion of that space by someone who is not closely related or invited can be very uncomfortable. If someone who you do not know invades your intimate space it is often because they are trying to intimidate you

☐ *personal or normal space* is what we like to maintain during our normal working or daily relationships with people we know. Strangers may need to be invited or accepted into that area. In certain situations, people's personal space will be reduced (for example, on crowded underground trains or in densely populated areas)

☐ *social or stranger space* is reserved for people we have not met before, and this is where your space as a steward will start. (You will need to try to maintain a distance of between 1 – 1.2 m (3 or 4 feet) in a conflict situation)

☐ *public space* is open space and is not considered a threat

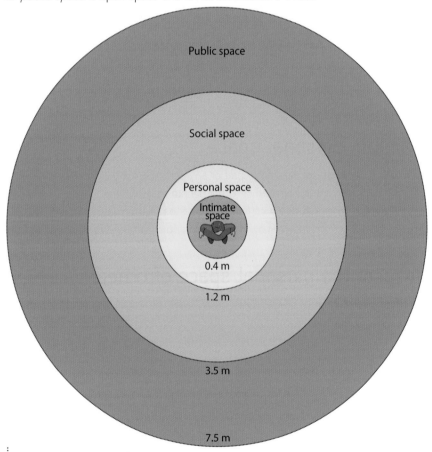

Figure 201.2 The four proxemic zones

The more we know about and respect the personal space of others, the more we can remain in control of any potential conflict situation. The illustrations above are averages and will vary depending on circumstances and culture.

Figure 201.3 Personal space is not affected at this distance

Figure 201.4 There is now a reaction due to the invasion of each other's space

Think about it

Write down why you think you should respect the personal space of others.

Can you write down examples of how you can remain safe and in control and start to defuse a conflict situation using personal space?

Active listening

Active listening is a technique which needs to be practised, and will show the customer that you are taking a genuine interest in what they are saying while acknowledging the issues they have. Your body language will show that you are listening and that you understand what they are saying. Nod your head to show understanding, repeat and summarise regularly what has been said and use occasional gestures and words to show that you are listening. If you check your understanding at every stage of the discussion, you will be able to maintain control of the situation and the customer will feel confident that you are paying attention and will be able to help.

While **actively listening**, try to use simple phrases to show that you understand their problem, for example:

- ☐ 'I can understand how you feel'
- ☐ 'I can see that this has made you annoyed'
- ☐ 'I'm sorry that you have had such a long wait.'

Key term

Active listening: showing that you are paying attention to what someone is saying, for example, by maintaining eye contact, nodding, asking further questions.

Active listening is a skill and takes practice

 Remember: The best way to show the customer that you are listening is to concentrate on the person and not be distracted by what is going on around you.

- Frequently show that you understand and say so.

- Summarise what has been said and then ask the person to continue.

- Use non-verbal signals and body language to show that you are listening.

- Keep using the right level of eye contact to show that you are listening and are not being distracted.

- Ask open questions which encourage full explanations, such as, 'Please tell me what happened', 'How did it happen?', 'What did you see?'.

- Be patient, allow the customer to talk and don't interrupt.

Show empathy

Empathy is another excellent conflict management technique. Showing empathy is not a sign of weakness: instead, it confirms that you understand how someone is feeling, which will increase their trust and confidence in you. This in turn will help to defuse and de-escalate the situation.

Empathy is not the same as sympathy. You are not feeling sorry for, and are not necessarily agreeing with, someone if you empathise with them. You are showing that you are human and putting yourself in their shoes, acknowledging that they have a view — and a right to that view — without necessarily agreeing with their view.

Showing empathy will allow you to remain in control of a situation and to be assertive when required. For example, you can make statements such as, 'I know you are annoyed because you have had a long wait in a queue, but if you continue to swear I will have no option but to ask you to leave this event. I don't want to have to do this.' If you remain calm and confident — and ensure your body language confirms this — you should be able to defuse most situations.

Sensitive questioning

People become angry and aggressive for a variety of reasons, some of which are not immediately apparent. In order to understand the reason for a person's irritation or complaint, you may have to ask a number of questions.

Sensitive questioning cannot take place unless you have built up a 'rapport' — an understanding with the customer. Listen actively, show empathy and understanding, be polite, calm and professional, and ensure your body language is confident and relaxed. If you do this, the customer is more likely to confide in you, and to have confidence in your ability to solve their problem.

Once you have won the customer's trust, you will be able to ask further questions and get them to explain anything that is unclear or confusing. Be patient and allow the person time to tell you in their own words what the problem is. It may be that the real cause of the problem is a personal issue which the customer is reluctant to talk about, especially in public. In this case, you will need to take the person to one side so you can speak to them quietly and confidentially.

As you can see, by the time you get to this point, the heat should have gone from the situation and people will be beginning to think rationally. The more information you have, the more likely it is that the problem will be resolved. The way to obtain more information is to ask open questions and listen carefully to the replies.

- Start with asking, who, what, where, when, why, how.

- Then move on to more detailed questions, such as, 'Are you saying that you are unhappy with _____ because _____?'

- Finally, try to get to the root of the problem by providing a number of possible answers and solutions, such as:

  - 'Are you saying it would help if we could _____?'

  - 'Am I right in thinking it would help you if we did _____?'

  - 'Would you like to be able to _____?'

> **Key term**
>
> **Sensitive questioning:** asking questions in a way that is not going to make the situation worse, for example, by being polite and phrasing questions so as not to upset someone.

Help to manage conflict Unit 201

Summarise and feed back to people

You need to know that the customer is satisfied with your solution to a problem and that the conflict is not going to re-occur.

Earlier in this section we discussed how to summarise at frequent intervals, so that the problem could be understood and the person could see that you were actively listening. It is equally important to close a problem with a summary and some feedback as to how the problem has been resolved.

If the customer agrees with your summary and feedback, you will have reached what is known as a 'win–win' situation. In other words, you both feel satisfied with the outcome and agree that the conflict is over.

You are satisfied because:

- you have found a good solution to the problem
- you have avoided conflict and stress
- others are satisfied with the outcome
- you have remained professional and calm at all times.

The customer is satisfied because:

- they have been listened to and taken seriously
- they have got what they needed without conflict
- the solution has not caused them any embarrassment in front of others
- they have been treated in a professional way.

Best Practice Checklist

- Always be aware that your attitude will affect your behaviour, which will then affect other people's attitude and behaviour.
- Be professional, make a good impression and use all your communication skills.
- Always understand and follow your organisation's procedures when dealing with conflict.
- Know and understand the law relating to the use of reasonable force.
- Be aware of the hotspots and triggers that can create a potential conflict situation.
- Know how to use, and practise using, active listening skills.
- Recognise blocks to communication and know how to deal with them.
- Think carefully before you enter anyone's personal space zones.
- Show empathy.
- Be aware that you may need to be discreet when asking sensitive questions.
- Always summarise and feed back to the customer to make sure that the problem has been dealt with.

Legal considerations – self-defence and the use of force

On rare occasions, you may need to defend yourself from being assaulted: in law this is known as self-defence and the use of force. If you have tried every communication and personal safety skill you have learnt and have not been able to resolve the situation, you need to know if you are protected by the law.

How could this steward deal with the situation?

The law is very clear. The Criminal Law Act 1967 (sec 3) states that:

'... a person may use such force as is *reasonable* in the circumstances in the prevention of crime, or in effecting or assisting in the lawful arrest of offenders or suspected offenders, or of persons unlawfully at large.'

You are not expected to make fine judgements over the level of force you use in the heat of the moment. So long as you only do what you honestly and instinctively believe is necessary at the time, you are acting lawfully and in self-defence. As a general rule, the more extreme the circumstances and the fear experienced, the more force you can lawfully use to defend yourself.

The law states that force may be used under certain circumstances to:

☐ defend oneself

☐ defend another person

☐ defend property

☐ make an arrest

☐ prevent a crime.

Table 201.3 shows the three important words that use of force should be based on:

Aspect	Questions to ask yourself
Reasonable (Criminal Law Act 1967 sec 3 (1))	● Did you honestly believe that force was the only option at the time? ● Would another reasonable person have held the same belief? ● Would another reasonable person have used that level of force in that situation?
Necessary (Defence of Necessity)	● Was the force used absolutely necessary? ● Was force stopped when no longer necessary? ● Was there another way of resolving the situation? ● Did you try anything else before resorting to force?
Proportionate	● Was the force used proportionate to the wrong it was stopping (avoiding)? ● Did you take into account the relative strength of the people involved, or the number of people involved? ● Did you consider training and experience, age and sex, and any weapons involved?

Table 201.3 Three important words to consider when using force

Your own role and responsibilities

Dealing with conflict is not one of your functions and should (unless absolutely necessary) be left to an SIA-licensed door supervisor or the police.

Your roles and responsibilities as an event steward relate to safety and customer care.

The *Guide to Safety at Sports Grounds* states that the ten basic duties of a steward are:

☐ to understand their general responsibilities towards the health and safety and welfare of all spectators, other stewards, ground staff and themselves

☐ to carry out safety checks

☐ to control or direct spectators who are entering or leaving the ground, and to help achieve an even flow of people to and from the viewing areas

☐ to assist in the safe operation of the ground, not to view the activity taking place

☐ to staff entrances, exits and other strategic points; for example, segregation, perimeter and exit doors or gates which are not continuously secured in the open position while the ground is in use

- to recognise crowd conditions so as to ensure the safe dispersal of spectators and the prevention of overcrowding, particularly on terraces or viewing slopes

- to assist the emergency services as required

- to provide basic emergency first aid

- to respond to emergencies (such as the early stages of a fire); to raise the alarm and take the necessary immediate action

- to undertake specific duties in an emergency or as directed by the safety officer or the appropriate emergency service officer.

Assess the risks of a situation

Whatever you do, or consider doing, in response to a possible conflict situation, you must think carefully about the consequences of your actions and avoid putting yourself or anyone else at risk. The way to do this is quite straightforward.

There will be procedures that you have agreed to follow and these will include a personal safety risk assessment for the event. Personal safety is a shared responsibility between your employer, the venue, your managers and yourself. The assessment will take account of the type of crowd expected at the event (for example, a local derby between two opposing football teams who have a reputation for violence at matches). This is known as crowd profiling.

Think about it

- Why do you need to stop and think about what you are doing before acting?
- How can you avoid putting yourself and others at risk?

What type of people and crowd would you expect at this sort of event?

Help to manage conflict Unit 201

The risk assessment will cover a number of main areas. The following example describes the process you might use at a football derby.

1. Identify the hazards

The personal safety hazards are likely to be a result of aggressive or violent activity, and/or the possession and use of prohibited/illegal items such as weapons, flares or bottles.

2. Identify the people who might be at risk during the event

- stewards
- police
- employees
- volunteers
- contractors
- vendors
- exhibitors
- performers
- members of the public (including children, elderly people, expectant mothers, disabled people, local residents and potential trespassers).

3. Identify the main points to consider

- type of event
- potential incidents and conflict
- site hazards
- type of crowd, control and segregation of crowd
- access and egress points
- capacity of the venue
- emergency services involvement
- first aid
- training – have the stewards been provided with the necessary training to recognise and manage personal safety and potential conflict?

4. Assess the risk

Once the hazards have been identified, the extent of the potential risk will need to be evaluated. The event managers will then need to decide whether the existing measures are sufficient or further measures are required. These measures could include:

- providing additional or more detailed information, instruction or training regarding the event and the potential activities
- ensuring that the event will fully comply with all legislation, codes of practice and British Standards.

5. Take further action to control the risk, if necessary

Key questions to ask are:

☐ Can the hazard be removed completely?

☐ Can access to the hazard be prevented?

☐ Can exposure to the hazard be reduced?

☐ Can personal protective equipment be provided?

6. Record your findings

All risk assessments – including decisions made and measures considered and implemented – have to be recorded. These records are known as 'key documents' and must be kept as they show that the event has been planned safely.

During the planning stages of an event, one of the main considerations will be the provision of a minimum number of stewards, based on the results of the risk assessment and other factors such as the crowd profile.

Inform the supervisor/control room of initial response

An early warning of an initial response to any incident is vital for providing you with support and advice, as well as monitoring the situation and making sure you are safe. Your colleagues will know what is happening and can observe from CCTV cameras, and/or simply keep an eye on the situation in case you need some help. Help can arrive in all sorts of ways depending on the scale of the incident; for example, you might need help with a person who has produced a ticket that could be forged, or you could be asking for help because of a large-scale pitch invasion.

Your communication will need to be clear, informative and accurate so that the scale of the initial response can be effective and realistic.

Maintain personal safety

There will be occasions when you need to maintain your own personal safety; as previously mentioned, this is a shared responsibility between your employer, the venue, your managers and yourself. When carrying out a risk assessment, you should always make a sensible judgement based on your training, the information and advice you have been given at the briefing, and the circumstances at the time.

Despite all the precautions, risk assessments, training and briefings that your employer has carried out with you, you may find yourself in a conflict situation which you need to prevent from escalating. You should employ all the techniques you have learnt: keep a safe distance; talk to the person; actively listen; show empathy; request assistance.

Functional skills

English: Speaking and Listening – your contribution to a discussion and the way that you communicate with people is important and will develop your speaking and listening skills

You must also carry on with the risk assessment. This is a personal safety risk assessment and will need to be dynamic (see page 92). If there is no time for planning in advance, you will need to concentrate on how the risk develops and how you can control it to yourself (and others).

The stages of a dynamic risk assessment are straightforward but will need to be practised.

- ☐ Stand back and think quickly about the risk.

- ☐ Assess the situation: do not rush to take immediate action.

- ☐ Think about the consequences of your actions – to yourself and others.

- ☐ Consider your options.

- ☐ Decide on the best course of action.

- ☐ Keep monitoring the situation and make a mental note of any changes.

- ☐ Ask yourself whether your decision is working, or whether you need to try another option.

Skills builder

Ask your colleagues if they have been involved in any potentially dangerous situations.

How did they deal with it?

Do they wish they had done anything differently?

Would you feel confident dealing with a similar situation?

> **!** **Remember:** Continue to monitor and assess the situation and circumstances as they change, adjusting your response as appropriate.

Best Practice Checklist

Dealing with difficult customers

- ☐ Maintain a positive and friendly attitude.

- ☐ Always treat customers with respect and courtesy.

- ☐ Create a smart, professional impression at all times.

- ☐ Always approach customers in a non-threatening manner.

- ☐ Never argue with anyone: if a situation is becoming difficult, contact your supervisor or control room immediately.

- ☐ Remember the 'Stewards' Code of Conduct'.

Collect and report information about the conflict and the people involved

After an incident, it is important to collect and record detailed information about what happened. You will need to find out about the people involved (victims, witnesses, suspects and alleged offenders) and the full story of what happened. Your initial report and any ongoing reports you make are invaluable to your colleagues and may well be recorded as evidence at a later stage. Your colleagues in the control room, as well as the emergency services and the managers of the event, will need to know exactly what you could see and hear.

It is important to remember when you write your report that the person reading it was not there, and so you need to paint a picture. In other words, what you write needs to explain logically and in sequence what you saw and heard. You should:

- plan what you are going to say
- plan a structure for your report
- make sure that what you write is legible and understandable
- never use a pencil to write the report
- never erase your work or use correcting fluid. If you have to make a correction, draw a line through the word or sentence and initial the correction.

When you write a report always make sure that it is accurate and unbiased

Best Practice Checklist ✓

Completing a pocket book or statement
A useful word to use when you complete your pocket book entry is ELBOWS — make sure your work contains no:

- **E** – erasures
- **L** – loose leaves
- **B** – blank spaces
- **O** – overwriting
- **W** – writing between lines
- **S** – slips of paper.

Remember to include who, what, when, where, how and why. Do not include your opinion — just state the facts and nothing else. For example, you should not say, *'The man I saw was drunk'*, because you may be asked how you know for certain he was drunk, rather than ill or suffering from an overdose of prescribed drugs. Instead, you could say, *'I could smell alcohol on Mr Jones' breath and he was slurring his speech and staggering.'*

The report must be signed and dated, to prove that you wrote it and so it can be used in court if required.

Think about it

If you don't write down what you saw and heard as soon as possible after it happened, how would you be able to remember it weeks or even months later?

Identify other sources of evidence

There are a number of other items of evidence that you might be able to provide other than documentary evidence, such as written reports contained within your pocket book, incident report or a formal witness statement.

Evidence can present itself in many ways. For example, at a crime scene there may be:

- physical evidence — a weapon, a package, clothing, bodily fluid such as blood, documents (e.g., an entrance ticket)

- witnesses — you need to identify any witnesses at the scene so that they can be interviewed and you can find out what they saw and heard

- digital evidence — for example, from photographs, CCTV recordings, mobile phones

- a suspect — the person who has been seen committing a crime may still be in the area and may even have admitted liability to you.

 Remember: It is very important to remember not to handle or move evidence, or to enter a crime scene.

Functional skills

English: Writing – When you write a report, you will be writing a detailed document in a logical sequence using suitable language, format and structure.

You can always ask your supervisor for help if you don't feel confident writing up a report

Working Life

Katie's story

I am a lecturer in customer care at a local college and also work part-time as an event steward. What I enjoy most is dealing with people and helping to sort out any problems.

Recently I found a man lying on the ground behind the hospitality tent. I thought at first he might be drunk and sleeping it off. I did a quick check and, although I could smell alcohol, I could see some blood on his head. I spoke to my supervisor and the control room, and as I was waiting for assistance the man got up and started swearing and shouting at me; he thought I had assaulted him. I used my skills in customer care, as well as carrying out a dynamic risk assessment. It turned out that someone had assaulted him and stolen his wallet.

Soon the man was receiving attention from a first aider as well as the police. As soon as I could, I wrote everything down in my pocket book and a few hours later I made a witness statement to the police about what had happened.

Ask the expert

Q What should I do if I haven't got a pocket book with me?

A You should always try to carry a pocket book and pen. If you do not have one, find some paper, put your name and date on the top, write your report and then sign and date it at the end. Keep this report safe for your supervisor, manager or the police.

Q Is being assertive different from being aggressive?

A Yes.

- Being assertive means being firm by directing and controlling a situation, and listening to the other person. Body language is confident and professional.

- Being aggressive often means a person is out of control – shouting, swearing and threatening and body language reflects this.

Top tips

✓ Never assume that a person is at fault because they are being aggressive: there could be an underlying medical or other reason.

✓ Ask for help from your supervisor as soon as possible.

✓ Carrying out a dynamic risk assessment will give you time to think and communicate.

✓ Make sure that you record the incident as soon as possible. Your report may be used in evidence at a later date.

Help to manage conflict Unit 201

Check your knowledge

1. What is the most important legal consideration covering the use of force and self-defence?

2. Why is it important to communicate with people in a conflict situation?

3. What is meant by the term 'personal space'?

4. Why is it important to show you are listening actively to what is being said?

5. Why is it important to show empathy?

6. Why should you inform the supervisor/control room of your initial response?

7. Why is it important to keep an accurate record of what has happened?

8. What does an authentic report mean?

9. State three different sources of evidence.

10. Which part of your communication is the most effective — the words that you speak, the tone of your voice or the non-verbal communication you use?

Getting ready for assessment

Once you have had some experience of dealing with different types of people, as well as of problems and conflict, you will be ready to be assessed towards this unit.

You will be observed communicating with people in conflict situations; your assessor will want to see that you are able to follow the organisation's procedures for dealing with conflict, especially how you remain calm while communicating in a way that minimises and reduces the risk and conflict. The assessor will also want to be sure that you know how to maintain personal space, actively listen to what people are saying, use empathy as well as sensitive questioning, and feed back to the people involved.

You will have to prove that you are able to assess risks, including the behaviour of people and how serious a situation is, while being able to maintain your own personal safety. You must be able to follow the procedures which state how you should deal with these situations as well as the people involved, while collecting and reporting the necessary information to the relevant people.

As well as being observed during this unit and expected to show how you would deal with conflict, so you will be asked to explain or describe why, how, or what makes the assessment criteria above so important. Most of this will be carried out with oral questions by the tutor.

Some of the evidence can also be obtained through the use of witness testimonies and personal records (for example a diary, pocket book, or a reflective account of what you have done).

If the evidence for learning outcomes 1 and 2 (Communicate with people in conflict situations; Follow procedures to resolve conflict) cannot be obtained at your place of work, your assessor may set up a realistic scenario to obtain the evidence through simulation.

Contribute to the work of the team

This unit is about how to work well as a member of a team while improving the way that you work and the work of the team as a whole.

The company that you work for and the organisation managing the venue must provide high levels of service to their customers – this requires team effort from all staff and managers. You will be expected to establish working relationships with colleagues, communicating with them clearly as you carry out your duties, and looking for feedback to help you improve your performance as well as the work of the organisation.

If your company has a performance appraisal and personal development system, this would be an excellent context for this unit.

You will learn how to:
- work effectively with colleagues
- improve your own work
- help improve the work of the organisation.

Work effectively with colleagues

Establish working relationships with colleagues

Key terms

Colleagues: the people you work with (those working at your own level and your managers).

Working relationship: the type of relationship with your colleagues that will help the team to work well and provide a high level of service to the customer; this includes getting along well with your colleagues, being fair to them, avoiding unnecessary disagreements and not letting your personal life influence the way you relate to colleagues.

Debrief: feeding back information relating to the way the event was managed and any incidents that occurred.

One of the first things anyone will notice about a team of people is whether or not the team is working well together. You will not work well together unless you know each other and what part you and your **colleagues** play within the team.

Remember: You are an important member of the team and the part you play is similar to a piece in a jigsaw puzzle. Without your contribution, the team will not work well.

These are the main ways you can establish an effective **working relationship** with your colleagues:

☐ Get to know your own and everyone else's experience, skills and knowledge. In this way you will know each other's strengths and weaknesses, understand who to support and who to ask for support.

☐ Be open and honest with each other. It is impossible to work well together without trust and good relationships. Any team – however large or small – relies on its members being open and honest about what they have done and what they are capable of doing.

☐ Help the other members of your team. Although you are always an individual with your own personality and abilities, you must be aware that teamwork cannot take place in isolation.

☐ Resolve any personal or team problems quickly and openly and have agreed methods for this. For example, you should plan how to respond if someone has to leave the team or if you have to manage an incident or other unexpected situation. A **debrief** on how well you work together will help to improve your individual and team performance.

☐ Keep your commitments to your colleagues. If you have a specific role within the team, the other members of the team will expect you to carry out this role and not leave it and start working on something else. You also have a commitment to your colleagues to report for duty on time so that you are a whole team, working together from the moment you arrive.

☐ Know your respective roles and responsibilities and what is expected of each other in the event of any incident your team has to deal with.

☐ Good leadership and methods of work are important aspects of effective team interaction (whether at work or play). Your managers and supervisors are part of the team that you work with; your roles and responsibilities have been put in place to plan who does what, when and how at the event.

Effective teamwork is not about individuals working well. It is about working together with your colleagues, including your supervisors and managers. Knowing who to help and support in your team and how to accept support when offered are key aspects of teamwork. A fully efficient team works together at the same pace and does not allow colleagues to fall behind.

When your team arrives at the event your purpose is to work together as a cohesive and organised unit. You should be proud to be a member of an effective team and your motivation, morale and work satisfaction should be high.

Communicate with colleagues

There are a number of qualities that, when combined, will provide the basis of a good team. One of these is communication with your colleagues. Without communication you will be working as individuals and not as a team. Good communication means being clear and concise, and providing the right amount of information, so there is no confusion about what you mean.

There will be times when you need to communicate with event stewards, supervisors, managers or safety officers. Under normal circumstances you should always commence the communication chain with your supervisor/control room,

Good communication is the foundation of efficient teams. How well do you communicate with your team?

but you may also need to communicate with other members of the team. For example, at a pre-event or post-event briefing, you may be asked to make comments or pose questions to your manager. The information you provide may be the part of the jigsaw that your manager needs to make an important decision.

Your contact with your managers in the team may be face to face, via a radio, or through a written report following an incident or accident. There are a number of reasons why you should always ensure that any communication, verbal or non-verbal, is clear and unambiguous.

- The people that you are communicating with need to understand exactly what you are going to do and what you want others to do. Never promise anything that you may not be able to achieve or is not going to happen.

- If people understand exactly what is going to happen, they are more likely to feel relaxed and at ease.

- If you are clear about what you have said or written, the person receiving the information is more likely to trust you.

- Misunderstandings can lead to confusion and disappointment, which may cause conflict.

- Clear communication will promote harmony within the team. Your colleagues will understand exactly what you mean and will trust your judgement.

- Clear communication will help to quickly resolve differences between people; telling the truth as you see it is a lot clearer than trying to make excuses.

- People often need to be instructed, especially in situations that involve conflict or during a security or safety incident. Clear instructions will be understood and acted upon.

Maintain standards of professional behaviour

In Unit 203 page 2, you learnt about standards of appearance and behaviour. All of these points are covered in the British Standard (BS 8406:2009) Event stewarding and crowd safety: Code of Practice, as well as in your organisation's policies and procedures. Together these documents set the standard for:

- events

- security personnel and safety officers

- crowd safety

- facilities for spectators, entertainment, sports etc.

- private enterprises

- contracts

- personnel management

- recruitment, job specifications, conditions of employment and working conditions (physical)

- training

- legislation

- records (documents).

Unit 203 page 2 also discussed standards of behaviour in relation to:

- manner and general conduct

- politeness, courtesy and helpfulness

- image, appearance, cleanliness and tidiness

- duties, roles and responsibilities

- attitude and behaviour

- eating, drinking and smoking in view of the public

- consuming alcohol or illegal substances before or during an event

- using obscene, offensive or intimidating language or gestures.

Your supervisors, managers of your company and the event organisers will monitor your standards frequently and give you feedback.

Carry out duties and commitments

In previous units you have looked at the duties you can be expected to carry out as an event steward (see Unit 205 Control the entry, exit and movement of people at spectator events, Unit 206 Monitor spectators and deal with crowd problems, Unit 201 Help to manage conflict) and how those duties and commitments are linked to your own personal roles and responsibilities within the team.

Your main duties and commitments are:

- to maintain the health and safety of yourself and others at the event

- to maintain good standards of customer care and help to make the event an enjoyable experience

- to carry out pre-event checks

- to provide essential information to the public and others (such as the emergency services) about the event and the venue's facilities

- to know the various codes and procedures in respect of emergencies and respond in a way that does not panic the public

- to respond to emergency situations by raising the alarm, reporting to supervisor/control room and assisting in an evacuation of the area if instructed to do so

☐ to provide assistance to casualty management if required to do so

☐ to assist the emergency services if required and when appropriate

☐ to assist in the control and flow of crowds and people

☐ to supervise spectators in your designated area

☐ to monitor and report any signs of overcrowding (the three 'Ds').

While at work your commitments are to your team, including the venue management, the people who work at the venue and the public at that event. If at any time you feel that you are unable to meet your commitments you must warn your colleagues that you cannot carry out your duties. It is important that your team is aware of any issues that may affect your performance on the day so that they can support you. This is because if the strength of the team is affected for any reason, this could have an overall effect on the health and safety of the whole event.

Ask for help and information

You will at times need to ask questions or ask for help, either due to lack of information or because the information is not clear. How many times, during meetings or in a classroom, have you wished you had more information but not asked because you thought your request was unimportant — only to find out later that other people were confused about the same issue? Asking for help and information is usually seen by colleagues — including managers — as a sign of strength and intelligence.

Don't be afraid to ask for help and information; others will also benefit from the answers

> **Think about it**
>
> Before you attend the next pre-event briefing or team meeting, write down three questions you want to use to contribute to the discussion. The questions will be for you to decide and might relate to:
>
> • your roles and responsibilities
> • how to deal with a communication issue within the team
> • training requirements
> • professional standards.

You may also find yourself in a situation when you need to request assistance from others in your team or from others. These situations will usually involve the health and safety of yourself or others, for example:

☐ potential conflict situations where you need the support of other members of your team (e.g. people trained and qualified in the use of physical intervention and disengagement skills) to help you deal with the problem

☐ an emergency incident where you will need the help of others to decide whether to evacuate or not.

Provide help and information

Your colleagues may ask you to provide help and information, so you will need to respond to their requests, for example:

- to help at the scene of an accident or incident

- to provide information regarding the layout or facilities at a venue

- to provide support in dealing with a potential conflict situation

- to manage the flow of a crowd.

However, there are some requests that you must not comply with because they may be illegal. For example, while you are contracted to carry out the role of an event steward, you should not complete any of the following tasks:

- guarding duties

- access control

- searching people (although please see pages 48–54 of Unit 205 for exceptions to this)

- physical intervention or disengagement

- ejection

- arrest and detention of individuals

- close protection.

Best Practice Checklist

Being an effective member of your team

- Get to know yourself, including your strengths and weaknesses.

- Get to know the other members of your team.

- Know your own and other team members' roles and responsibilities.

- Be honest with yourself and with all members of the team.

- Help everyone whenever possible.

- Never let problems or issues fester: deal with any interpersonal problems quickly.

- Make commitments and keep to them.

- Maintain a high standard of appearance and behaviour.

- Never be embarrassed or afraid to ask for help or ask questions.

- Become involved in team meetings and discussions whenever possible.

- Communicate, communicate, and communicate.

Contribute to team discussions

Discussions with your team will usually take place:

☐ immediately following the main event briefing

☐ after an incident

☐ at the event debriefing.

As an important and integral member of the team you will be expected to take part in and contribute to the discussion, passing on information based on your previous knowledge or experience, or gained by observing or communicating with people in your designated area. By contributing to discussions and sharing information in a supportive environment, you can improve the efficiency and effectiveness of the whole operation and therefore the health, safety and wellbeing of everyone at the event.

Team meetings can take place anywhere, for example, in the designated area before the event or in a meeting room, but preferably in an environment free from interruption and noise. During these meetings, you will have the opportunity to ask questions about any issues you have encountered or may encounter in the future. Asking these questions will allow the team to plan for — and hopefully prevent — incidents. This is often a lot more effective than telling people of their duties via email. For instance, if one or more members of the team did not act effectively during an incident, you can plan an alternative strategy to ensure that this does not happen again.

Team meetings therefore also allow you to review and improve your performance, both as individuals and as a team. Remember, an effective team is one that works well together and allows full and free communication at all levels.

Functional skills

English: Speaking, listening and communication — By contributing to discussions, explaining things clearly and actively listening, you will be developing your speaking and listening skills.

Follow the correct procedures when disagreements or difficulties arise

There may be occasions when disagreements and difficulties arise within your team. Not everyone will agree with what you are saying or doing all of the time, and this could lead to difficulties between yourself and others and a possible breakdown of cooperation within the team.

Your company will have a procedure to make sure that any disagreements or difficulties in the team, or between individuals, are dealt with quickly, so you must report any concerns to your supervisor who will try to deal with it and resolve the issue. If this process does not work then the issue will be referred to the management, who will then make a decision.

There are also policies and procedures that cover specific issues of conflict within a team that team members and supervisors need to be aware of, such as when a member of the team fails to follow the Code of Conduct.

Team meetings are a good way of sharing information and building team relationships

Grievance procedure

A grievance means 'a concern, problem or complaint' and is usually raised by an employee to their employer about an issue that the employee feels strongly about and would like to be dealt with. Your employer should have a policy and procedure which has been communicated to you, which you should be able to get from:

- ☐ your stewards' handbook
- ☐ your employment contract
- ☐ your company's intranet site
- ☐ your company's HR (Human Resources) department.

If possible and appropriate, try to get the grievance dealt with informally at first by talking to your supervisor or manager.

Appeals procedure

If you are not satisfied with the result of a complaint you have made, or if you feel you have been disciplined unfairly, your employer will have a process for you to appeal against the decision.

Disciplinary procedure

Your employer will have a policy on how the company deals with disciplinary matters, including a procedure for letting you know that your performance or conduct is not up to the standard expected of an event steward. Unless the matter is very serious, your employer may simply talk to you about your performance and give you the chance to explain yourself in case there has been a misunderstanding, in which case your explanation may be all that is required.

The way in which your employer deals with discipline and dismissal issues will be written down and provided to you when you join the company.

If the matter is dealt with formally it is likely to involve the following steps:

- a letter from your employer setting out the issue
- a meeting with your employer to discuss the issue
- the opportunity to appeal against your employer's decision.

Violence in the workplace

The Health and Safety Executive (HSE) issues a guide for employers on the subject of violence at work, which can be found on their website (for a link to the HSE website please visit www.pearsonhotlinks.com). It is aimed at people who deal directly with the public and who may face aggressive or violent behaviour, including being sworn at, threatened or even attacked.

The work that an event steward is expected to perform falls within the above definition, so it is very likely that your employer will have a written policy on how the company deals with violence in the workplace and to their employees.

Remember that your supervisors and managers will apply the correct procedure should there be a need to do so.

Improve your own work

Evaluate your work

You should strive continuously to improve your performance, ability and skill. Personal and professional development will allow you to progress at work and improve the overall performance of your team organisation.

There are a variety of ways in which you can improve and develop. For example, you might find that direct experience (doing it yourself – acting, sensing and feeling) is the best way to learn, while others might prefer to observe someone at work and think about it before going in at the deep end!

Think about it

How do you find it easiest to learn at work? Do you prefer to learn by direct experience or by observation and reflection? Let your trainer or supervisor know your preferred learning methods.

It is important to review and **evaluate** your work and performance so you and your team can continue to improve.

Self-assessment and evaluation are very important. You should know instinctively whether you have done well or could have done better; by asking yourself various key questions, you will become more aware of your own competence and performance and will learn to see yourself as others might see you.

One of the best ways to monitor your performance at work is to keep a reflective journal, diary or account of your experiences and how you dealt with any issues. Write down your feelings, and how you could improve or change the way you approach people or problems at work.

Key term

Evaluation: thinking about your work and identifying what you do well and how you could improve.

Action
What did I do today at the event?
Objectives
What did I hope to achieve at the event today?
Outcomes
How did I really do? Did I meet my objectives?
Opportunities
What could I have done differently? How would this have affected the outcomes?
Constraints
What prevented my actions from being as successful as they might have been? What could I do about this?
Future actions
What will I do differently as a result of this experience?

Figure 202.1 An example of a reflective account form

Ask colleagues and customers for feedback

See if you can share some of your thoughts with your colleagues or supervisor. See if their **feedback** matches your own assessment and identify any important differences of opinion.

Try to be as honest with yourself as possible. The sooner you accept yourself (including the things that you would rather others didn't know about) the sooner you will feel comfortable about allowing others to become involved in the assessment process. To reach your true potential, you need to know what others really think about you (not necessarily the things that you want to hear), accepting this as positive feedback and using it to build and plan your future development. All of this will help you perform more effectively and become more professional in the way you work.

You may also receive formal or informal feedback from customers. Informal feedback is usually received when customers make comments to you about the way in which they have been dealt with or how they felt while at the event.

Key term

Feedback: comments from other people (customers or colleagues), telling you what they think.

Asking other people for honest feedback on your work can be a really useful starting point when evaluating your own performance

Formal feedback is usually provided through a survey questionnaire, letter, telephone call or email.

When you receive feedback from a customer, either report it to your organisation through their formal recording and reporting systems and processes, report it at the debriefing, or discuss it with your supervisor who will feed back to the management.

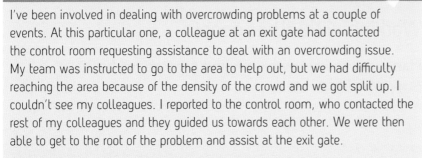

Case study

I've been involved in dealing with overcrowding problems at a couple of events. At this particular one, a colleague at an exit gate had contacted the control room requesting assistance to deal with an overcrowding issue. My team was instructed to go to the area to help out, but we had difficulty reaching the area because of the density of the crowd and we got split up. I couldn't see my colleagues. I reported to the control room, who contacted the rest of my colleagues and they guided us towards each other. We were then able to get to the root of the problem and assist at the exit gate.

Over to you

How could you and your team use this experience to improve on the work that you do? You should ask the following questions and answer them in a logical way.

- ☐ What happened?

- ☐ Why did it happen?

- ☐ What can I learn for next time so I can improve?

- ☐ Is there an opportunity or need for further training?

Handle constructive criticism positively

All criticism, if given in the right way and for the right purpose, should be positive and meaningful. The worst kind of criticism is the type that is negative to you and to the team in general. Positive feedback is provided to you for the right reasons and, if taken in a positive frame of mind, will help you and the team improve your performance.

For example, the safety officer who monitors the way in which you and your team carry out safety checks in your designated area might comment: 'I know that you cover the same area every week and are all experienced stewards, but you are not checking everything as carefully as you should. I followed behind you and found some rubbish in the seating area, two broken chairs and a barrier that was not fixed properly. Please try to make sure everything is checked properly as this is a very important health and safety requirement.'

This is constructive criticism and very positive; the safety officer is acknowledging the experience of the team and that you all know how to carry out the role, but is criticising the team as a whole (not an individual) for not working properly and pointing out the reasons why. The team should deal with the criticism during the debriefing.

In this example, the safety officer is likely to receive a positive response from the team who will remember the advice in future and act on it.

> **Think about it**
>
> Make a note of how you will handle criticism and consider:
> - how you can turn any criticism into positive feedback
> - how you can use the feedback to your advantage and future development.

Working with other people

Plan ways to improve work and prepare for future responsibilities

When you work closely with a team, there are times when you will receive help, support and advice, both from your supervisor and from other members of the team.

Within your team or organisation someone will be responsible for you, helping you to plan and develop your work. This person will differ from organisation to organisation. For example, it could be your:

- ☐ training manager
- ☐ HR manager
- ☐ supervisor
- ☐ chief steward
- ☐ operations manager
- ☐ safety officer.

> **Key term**
>
> **Future responsibilities:** these could be new duties that you want to take on or new duties that your line manager wants to give you. This could include promotion.

> **Think about it**
>
> You will need to work with someone who will help you plan your work and prepare you for **future responsibilities**.
> - Think about what future responsibilities you would like to take on.
> - Find out who in your organisation can help you to achieve your aims.
> - Meet this person and discuss your options.

When you are confident and experienced enough to provide your colleagues with constructive and positive feedback, you will become a more valuable member of the team. Earlier, you learnt how important it is to accept honest feedback and to analyse your own strengths and weaknesses. You should also be able to carry this out with members of your team when you meet and discuss individual and team performance.

For example, you may have noticed that a member of the team finds it difficult to carry out certain tasks, such as searching the seating area at the top of a designated area. (Some stadiums are very high and acrophobia (fear of heights) is a common condition.) Within the team, this problem could be solved very easily by offering to carry out searches of higher seating areas yourself, so they don't have to.

Think about what responsibilities you might like to take on in the future, and how you might prepare yourself for them

Identify new areas of skill and knowledge that may be needed for future responsibilities

In order to assist your continued development, you will need to think about your future career progression. Think about what role you would like to progress to: maybe event team supervisor, team leader, security guard, chief steward, deputy or safety officer (if you think you are particularly good at interacting with people and have a flair for calming down customers), and the skills and training you will need.

Once you have identified the role, ask your supervisor if you could be put forward for the training.

Identify strengths and areas for improvement

Recognising your own areas of strength, as well as those of the team as a whole and of individual team members, means you will instantly know who to turn to when you need support. Likewise, acknowledging weaknesses and talking openly with your supervisor will enable the team to work on those areas and become more effective.

 Remember: The more open and honest everyone is about their strengths and weaknesses, the easier it is to give and accept constructive feedback.

Skills builder

Working with other members of your team to help them plan and improve their performance is a skill which requires good interpersonal techniques and a positive attitude.

- Talk to your supervisor about how much input you can have during meetings.

- Know the limits of your job role and be aware of what you can and cannot do when helping other team members.

- Make sure that other members of the team are at a stage where they not only accept feedback but can also give the same feedback to others.

Skills builder

Your ongoing **training and development** is important not only for you and your team but also for your company and the venue.

- Ask about the content of induction training.

- Keep a record of what you have achieved and find out what other training your company can provide for you.

- Ask if you can complete any on-the-job training, such as an NVQ.

- Keep a record of the different types of events that you attend, different roles that you undertake and any other activities that show personal development (e.g. practising new skills, observing other members of staff at work, receiving instructions, etc.).

Key term

Training and development: this could involve a course, watching other members of staff doing things that are new to you and receiving instructions from them, or having the opportunity to practise new skills.

Training and development

Every organisation will have a different training and development procedure, which you should discuss with your supervisor or manager when given feedback or a personal appraisal. The training and development policy will often depend on the size of the company and the resources it has for training activities.

Your personal record, held by your employer, will include a list of your training. These records are often requested by event managers as evidence that you have received appropriate and sufficient training to carry out your roles and responsibilities.

You might also want to consider keeping your own record of training as a personal development record, showing the training and qualifications you already hold and those you would like to achieve during the next few years. If your company has a list of training courses or you know of other courses that would help you develop, ask your supervisor or raise the question at a briefing.

Table 202.1 shows a list of some of the training and development programmes you might be able to undertake.

Training programme	Level
Understanding Stewarding at Spectator Events	Level 2: a good introduction to the roles and responsibilities of an event steward
NVQ Certificate in Spectator Safety	Level 2: on-the-job training and assessment which assesses your knowledge, understanding and competence to carry out the job of an event steward
NVQ Certificate in Spectator Safety	Level 3: on-the-job training and assessment which assesses your knowledge, understanding and competence to carry out the job of an event steward supervisor. Suitable for people who are already involved in that role or who wish to show potential as a supervisor
NVQ Certificate in Spectator Safety Management	Level 4: on-the-job training and assessment which assesses your knowledge, understanding and competence to carry out the role of manager of stewarding operations for spectator events
Customer Care	Various levels of vocational programmes, suitable for event stewards, supervisors and managers
Door Supervision and Physical Intervention	Level 2: suitable for event stewards whose role requires additional 'security' activities as laid down by the Private Security Industry Act
Security	Level 2: suitable for people involved in event security, for example patrol, guarding, access control, conflict management or searching persons
Close Protection	Level 3: suitable for people whose role is to protect the safety and security of VIPs who attend events
First Aid	Various levels of programmes suitable for all people involved in spectator safety and security duties

Table 202.1 Possible training and development programmes

Review personal development

Previously you learnt about the importance of training and development as well as that of keeping a record of your activities. It is equally important to carry out a regular review of your training and development plan to check and monitor whether or not you are meeting your objectives. This will also help you to re-focus your thoughts on your original plan to see if you are continuing to develop, if there are any gaps and whether or not your plans are still achievable.

Table 202.2 shows an example of a PDP (Personal Development Plan) with a review of the objectives.

My objectives	*I want to qualify as a Door Supervisor*
Can I break this down into small steps?	• *See if there is a local course I can go on: ask my friend (who is a door supervisor), ask my supervisor or look on the web.* • *Find the time to do the course – plan ahead.* • *Find out how much it will cost. Where will I get the money? Will my company help me pay?* • *Find out whether there are additional costs for the licence.*
What skills do I need to accomplish this?	• *Finding information* • *Time management* • *Preparing a case for the course to be funded* • *Application of knowledge and understanding* • *Practical skills required for the role of a door supervisor*
When will I have accomplished it?	• *I want to achieve and qualify by April.* • *I want to obtain my SIA Door Supervisor's Licence by May.*
Did I make the deadline?	*No*
If not, what went wrong?	• *I found out that the course would cost £400 and the licence would cost additional £245. I would need to take 5 days off work without pay to complete the training, so in total, the qualification would cost about £1200.* • *I cannot afford this yet – I have a young family and my employer will not help with the cost of training.*
How can I prevent this from happening next time?	• *Be more realistic about work and financial demands.* • *Save the money required and put it into a separate account to pay for the training. It will be a worthwhile investment as I will earn more money at events and I will be able to get part-time work as a door supervisor.*

Figure 202.2 An example of a PDP form

Functional skills

English: planning a PDP, organising it into sections, checking your work for grammar, punctuation and spelling errors and writing a final draft will help develop your English and writing skills.

A PDP provides a great opportunity to discuss your performance with your manager and get feedback

Best Practice Checklist

How to improve your own work

- ☐ Never stop learning.

- ☐ Monitor and analyse your personal development and performance.

- ☐ Keep a reflective journal, diary or account of what you do and think about how you could improve.

- ☐ Be honest with yourself and with others and they will be honest with you.

- ☐ Look for feedback from colleagues and customers on your performance.

- ☐ Look forward to all feedback, including constructive criticism, and use it to develop.

- ☐ Report any feedback to your company so that it can be used to improve performance.

- ☐ Start to set your own objectives for training and keep a plan of what you want to achieve

- ☐ Establish a personal development plan.

Help improve the work of the organisation

Ask customers for feedback on the services the organisation provides

Most organisations take feedback from customers seriously and use it to monitor, analyse and improve the service they provide. Customer feedback is important because all businesses need to retain customers and their loyalty. For some reason, previously happy customers may stop attending a certain venue and move their loyalty elsewhere, even if it means more inconvenience for them. Most of these customers will never complain or tell you why — unless you ask them.

You will find many opportunities to ask customers for their feedback relating to service and customer satisfaction level:

☐ in queues

☐ in your designated area

☐ at facilities such as toilets and refreshment areas

☐ after dealing with a customer problem or incident.

At intervals during the year you might also be asked to collect information from customers via a form, which can be completed quickly and handed to your supervisor at the end of the event. This may include questions that ask:

☐ Does the customer think that there is anything that needs to be done differently?

☐ What does the customer say about how well the organisation is meeting customer needs and expectations?

☐ How did the customer feel when they arrived at the event, and during and after the event?

☐ How many customer complaints or compliments were made at the event?

☐ What do customers think about the behaviour and attitudes of the event stewards?

Lastly, ask an open-ended question (e.g. How could we develop our services?). This provides the customer with an opportunity to state what they disliked or to make useful and positive suggestions that could help the business to develop.

There will also be opportunities when stewards and their managers can feed back information from customers to each other and the organisation. These opportunities may present themselves during:

☐ pre-event preparation

☐ event activities

☐ post-event debrief.

Skills builder

Asking customers for feedback requires you to be positive, friendly and motivated, showing a genuine interest in what they have to say.

- Ask your supervisor about how your company obtains feedback from customers.

- Ask to see a customer feedback form and identify the main information your company is collecting to monitor and analyse its customer care performance.

- Ask if you can take some forms with you and complete them with customers.

- Make suggestions if you think that the feedback form needs amending.

Identify ways in which the team could improve the organisation's services to customers

Exceptional customer service involves the whole team, not just you as an individual. One weak link in the team can turn a customer's good experience into a negative one, and may well result in a complaint or prompt the customer to go elsewhere in the future. It is therefore very important that each member understands their role and works with the rest of the team to create a good impression and look after the needs of customers at all times.

Here are some ways in which you and your team could improve the organisation's services to customers.

Employing the right people

Your organisation should make sure that it employs the right sort of people. This may sound simplistic, but personality, attitude and behaviour count for a great deal. Nice people who are friendly and like to meet and talk to others are usually good ambassadors and are empathetic to customers' needs, helping to solve problems and wanting everyone to enjoy themselves.

Training

Your company should provide ongoing staff training in customer service skills, using life-like scenarios based on real situations and customer issues that you are likely to face.

Customer feedback

Your company and the venue should make sure that you and the rest of your team understand the reason for customer feedback, and that all members are motivated and positive when collecting the information. The organisation must ensure that they act on the results of feedback and share this with you.

 Remember: Always approach customers and ask for feedback in a friendly and positive way. Your motivation and interest in what they say is important to them and to your company.

Suggest improvements to colleagues

Never feel embarrassed or afraid to make suggestions, no matter how small or trivial you think they are. Ideas about how to improve the way in which a company operates often come from people on the 'coal face' — people like you, event stewards carrying out the customer-facing role at each event.

Your company should have procedures in place to collect suggestions from their staff, for example:

- face to face with your supervisor

- at team meetings and briefings

- via a suggestion box

- via the intranet

- via email.

Actively listening to customers can also provide the basis for good ideas. If a customer suggests a way to improve things, it is usually because they have been to other events and have seen better processes working.

Examples of suggestions put forward by customers and event stewards are numerous and include those for people waiting in queues:

- provide advance traffic information by text so customers can avoid congestion and find a suitable car park

- provide information on waiting times in a queue

- provide refreshments for people in the queue (especially in hot weather)

- have cheap plastic raincoats available for sale if it rains.

None of the above suggestions would cost much (if anything) for your company to put in place, but would certainly improve comfort levels, customer service and satisfaction for everyone waiting to enter the event.

If you have a suggestion box at your venue, find out who is responsible for monitoring and acting on the suggestions

Think about it

Write a list of the occasions when you think that customer care could have been improved. Think about the following areas or situations:

- entering the venue/queuing to enter
- car parking facilities
- searches on entry
- providing assistance
- refreshments and toilet facilities.

Now write a list of possible solutions to improve customer care.

Functional skills

English: writing down a list of suggested improvements to customer care, planning and amending a questionnaire and assisting customers to complete it, writing a report on ways to improve customer care and checking your work for grammar, punctuation and spelling errors will help improve your English writing skills.

Discuss how improvements could be put into practice

You should always try to contribute as much as possible to any **team discussions**, which will help to improve the effectiveness and professionalism of your team and the organisation. These discussions will allow you to listen to the opinions and thoughts of more experienced stewards and supervisors and to learn from what they are saying. They will also give you an opportunity to put your improvement suggestions forward and ask for them to be discussed.

Key term

Team discussions: these will usually be team meetings but could include more informal discussions with team members and line managers.

Unit 202

Contribute to the work of the team

Remember that effective and efficient teams work best if people communicate and are allowed to express their opinions and thoughts openly without fear of embarrassment. All members of the team should work within a positive and confident environment which allows for healthy and positive discussions.

What improvements could your team make?

Best Practice Checklist

How to obtain feedback and make suggestions

☐ Look for opportunities to get feedback from customers.

☐ Collect all information from customers in a positive and friendly manner.

☐ Show that you are interested in what the customer is saying and actively listen to suggestions.

☐ The whole of your team must work hard to improve customer care; the weakest link is the person in the team who is not interested.

☐ Never feel embarrassed or afraid to make suggestions which might improve the work of your company.

☐ Try to get involved by making suggestions and taking part in discussions at team meetings and briefings.

Working Life

Adam's story

I work as an event steward at the UK's biggest arena, where my role is with a team who meet and greet people.

We try to make people feel welcome to put them in the right frame of mind. The first year, two of the team members acted more like security guys, instructing customers where to go in an unfriendly way. I had a chat with one of them and asked if we could change partners so we could all get to know each other better. He agreed, so I put the suggestion to my supervisor and next time found myself working with one of them. It was interesting to see how different he was when working with me — his whole attitude changed and he soon became a really friendly person, doing the same job in a different way.

It was good to see how straightforward it was to make a suggestion that improved the way in which colleagues and the team worked together.

Ask the expert

Q I am concerned about the assessment criterion which states that I should know when not to provide help and information to my colleagues. Surely I should always provide help?

A Ultimately this is a decision for you to make. If the situation is very serious (a colleague or members of the public are in danger or being attacked), you may be able to justify assisting someone even if you are not licensed to do so. However, if a colleague or supervisor asks you to do something you are not licensed to do (e.g. help eject or search people), you and your company could be prosecuted.

Q What if I have a problem with my supervisor? I worked with a supervisor once who was a bully: no one liked them and I was scared to say anything.

A Remember you are part of a large team, which your supervisor and managers are also part of. If you are concerned about the actions of a supervisor, you should speak to a manager.

Top tips

✓ Always try to resolve any issues within the team in a way which will create a 'win–win' situation for everyone involved.

✓ Never be afraid or embarrassed to make suggestions.

✓ Be honest with yourself and with your feedback to others. They will repay you with honesty.

Check your knowledge

1 What is meant by the term 'values and codes of practice' relevant to the work of an event steward and where will you find these?

2 Why is effective teamwork important?
a) It ensures you know who is working in the company.
b) It ensures better pay for all employees.
c) It ensures you can work well on your own.
d) It ensures high quality and professional standards for individuals, the team and the company.

3 What are 'effective working relationships' with your colleagues?

4 How would you establish effective working relationships with your colleagues?

5 How do you communicate with managers in your organisation during an event?
a) by using a loud speaker
b) through the chain of command
c) by leaving your area to go and speak to them
d) by emailing them.

6 Why is it important to carry out your duties as agreed or to warn colleagues in good time if you cannot?

7 In which situations may you need help in your work and why should you always ask for help and information in these situations?

8 In which situations should you NOT provide help and information to your colleagues?

9 Why are team discussions important and why should you contribute to them?

10 Why is it important to listen to customer feedback?

Getting ready for assessment

Once you feel confident working with your colleagues, you will need to show that you understand how to improve your work as well as the work of the organisation. You will then be ready for assessment.

You will have to prove you can work effectively with different types of colleagues, for example:

- team members who are working at the same level as yourself

- people who are responsible to you

- your line manager.

You will have to show that you have spoken to them and communicated with them in writing (e.g. via a report or memo).

You will also need to show evidence that you are improving your own work and the work of the organisation in a way that involves the colleagues listed above. You will have another opportunity to provide evidence when you talk to your assessor and answer questions orally and/ or in writing.

Unit 204

Deal with accidents and emergencies

In this unit you will learn what your roles and responsibilities are if you are involved in situations involving minor injury or illness, or even a major evacuation. As the first person on the scene your response is often vital, so it is important that you know how to react quickly and effectively should an emergency arise. This will include learning emergency procedures at the venue and how to assist in evacuating crowds from the area. You will also learn how to respond to and manage casualties during an incident requiring medical assistance or first aid. You will not need medical skills to do this but your initial actions could save lives.

You will learn how to:

☐ deal with injuries and signs of illness
☐ follow emergency procedures.

Deal with injuries and signs of illness

Injuries and illnesses that may occur in your area of work

At any event involving large numbers of people, there is a high risk of injury or illness. The most common problems are shown in Table 204.1.

Possible injuries	Possible illnesses
Choking	Fainting
Collapse	Unconsciousness
Bleeding	Hypertension
Bruising	Cardiac arrest
Crush asphyxia	Epilepsy
Broken bones	Shock
Burns	Vomiting
Hypothermia can be caused by cold weather, torrential rain	Panic attack
Hyperthermia can be caused by sun stroke	Drug or alcohol overdose
Sprains	Nosebleed
Cuts and scratches	Sore throat
Stab wound	Diabetes

Table 204.1 Typical injuries or illnesses

Think about it

Look at the list above and decide which illnesses and injuries need to be dealt with by the emergency services and which could be dealt with by a qualified first aid person.

- Which would be considered minor injuries or illnesses?
- Which would be considered major injuries or illnesses?

Key terms

Hypothermia: excessive reduction in body temperature.

Hyperthermia: excessive increase in body temperature

Values and codes of practice

The values and codes of practice for event stewarding and therefore for the work that you do (including dealing with accidents and illnesses) are clearly laid out in various documents, including those produced by:

☐ Health and Safety Executive (HSE) – *Emergency First Aid* and *First Aid at Work*

☐ your organisation's policies and procedures

☐ the event safety plan

☐ British Standard (BS 8406:2009) *Event stewarding and crowd safety: Code of Practice*.

What injuries and illnesses might you expect to find at an event such as this?

Deal with accidents and emergencies

It is essential to deal with any accident or emergency professionally: you must act promptly, calmly and correctly (by following procedures).

At the scene of the accident, you will need to report to your supervisor immediately, providing initial information about:

☐ the extent of the injury or illness

☐ the response required

☐ whether the cause of the injury or illness is likely to affect anyone else at the venue.

By reporting and dealing with the incident in a professional way, you will be:

☐ preventing any further danger

☐ preserving life

☐ promoting recovery

☐ preventing panic.

At all times you will be managing the situation until qualified help arrives.

You also need to carry out a risk assessment when you arrive at the scene of an accident or illness. Consider and assess:

☐ the immediate area — is it safe?

☐ the cause of the injury or illness — is it still present and is anyone else at risk?

☐ the casualty — are they in danger of further injury or of injuring anyone else?

- the casualty's friends or colleagues — are they in danger or likely to be a risk?

- other people in the area — are they in danger of further injury or of injuring anyone else?

- yourself and your colleagues — is it safe for you to carry out your role?

Follow the organisation's procedures

Your organisation will provide procedures that clearly outline what you need to do in case of an injury or illness while at work. This information will be part of the event organisers' and safety officers' safety plan, for which you will receive full guidance during the pre-event briefing. You should also find the information in the steward's handbook, but it is also advisable to make notes during the briefing of any important procedures specific to your venue.

A typical safety plan for a music event (other types of event follow the same type of format) will follow the guidance contained within the HSE publication *HSG 195 — The Event Safety Guide*, and will hold all the information required to ensure that the health, safety and welfare of those attending the event, including employees and contractors, are managed.

You probably won't have time to read the plan, but it is useful to know that it exists and that it outlines your roles and responsibilities during an emergency. It should contain:

- roles and responsibilities of people given safety duties (such as the safety officer and event stewards) and the person responsible for all safety at the event

- a description of the event and the likely numbers of people attending, together with maximum occupancy figures for specific areas and the venue as a whole

- a full risk assessment

- an event timeline, from start to finish

- details of muster points, first aid facilities etc.

- the level of support from other organisations such as the **emergency services**, voluntary organisations and the local authorities

- fire safety arrangements, including roles and responsibilities of event stewards, fire marshals and emergency services

- first aid arrangements such as trained first aiders, first aid equipment, voluntary organisations and emergency services

- emergency evacuation and egress for disabled and/or people with particular requirements

- communication methods — with stewards, managers, organisers, emergency services and the public

Functional skills

English: Reading and writing — reading and understanding your organisation's procedures for dealing with injury or illness, and writing down important points for your role will help develop your English reading and writing skills.

Key term

Emergency services: usually the fire service, ambulance service or police.

- transport management such as evacuation of car parks and the segregation of vehicles from pedestrians
- contingency plans for major incidents such as acts of terrorism, fire, flood or building collapse.

Deal with injuries and illnesses until qualified assistance arrives

You should only apply first aid techniques if you are qualified to do so: never try to use first aid unless you know how to. Your role is casualty management, so you need to carry out an initial risk assessment and report what you have found to your line manager.

1 Check for immediate dangers and remove hazards if it is safe to do so

Possible dangers or hazards include:

- slips and trips from obstructions on the ground, water, mud, ice etc.
- falling from height (walls, staircases)
- weather conditions
- crowd density (too many people in one area)
- crowd dynamics.

2 Ensure that the area is safe so there are no more injuries

- Seal off the area.
- Request assistance from colleagues if necessary.
- Request help from a cleaner or facilities to remove water/put down grit on ice etc.

3 Take care of any casualties

- Check for a response from the patient.
- Establish medical information by finding out what happened or if there is a history of illness.
- Get help by contacting your supervisor or control room.
- Stay calm and reassure the patient if possible.
- Keep people around you calm and away from the patient.

4 Before qualified assistance arrives, maintain control

Continuously monitor the circumstances, for example:

- the patient(s)
- the incident
- the people in the area.

5 If possible, obtain the following details:

☐ full name

☐ date of birth

☐ address

☐ next of kin

☐ contact number (e.g. for a relative, friend, carer etc.)

☐ details of any vehicles or equipment on site.

6 Inform the qualified medical staff/first aider about:

☐ what happened

☐ when the incident occurred

☐ who is involved.

Be prepared to assist the qualified person if asked, but remember to contact your supervisor/control room and inform them of the request for you to assist. Never compromise your stewarding role – if you do so, you may put more lives at risk.

The importance of protecting the casualty

If a spectator in a crowd is injured or seriously ill, you will need to assess the situation and report back to your supervisor or to the control room. You may not be a qualified first aider but you may be able to provide assistance. All casualties should be protected from further harm or injury. If there is one casualty there is a risk that others could be injured. Remember the three 'R's:

☐ **Remove** the casualty from the scene (if it is safe to do so) or remove any external danger.

☐ **Restrict** the entry of people to the area.

☐ **Report** the circumstances to your supervisor/control room as soon as possible.

The letters 'DRABC' should also help you.

☐ **D – Danger:** Check the area and make sure that you are safe and the people around you are in no danger.

☐ **R – Response:** Can the casualty hear your voice? Can they open and close their eyes? Are they moving? Do they respond to touch?

☐ **A – Airway:** Is there a blockage in the casualty's throat or have they swallowed their tongue? Is the head in a suitable position (check first aid manual for details) to aid breathing? Care should be taken not to make anything worse but the airway **MUST** be cleared if it is blocked.

☐ **B – Breathing:** Can the casualty breathe? Once the airway is clear, is there any other problem – the lungs, for example?

☐ **C – Circulation:** Is there a pulse? Is the heart beating? Is the pulse weak/strong/racing?

When you have reported back to your chain of command, you must remember the three 'P's:

- **Protect** the casualty from further risk: clear the area as much as possible by making space around the injured/ill person. If the person is bleeding badly, apply pressure to stop the flow of blood. Remember that the object or person that caused the injury may still be close by and it is very important to protect the **casualty** from immediate risk.

- **Preserve** life: if the person is seriously injured/ill, do whatever you can to keep them alive until **qualified assistance** arrives. You will need to ensure that the casualty's airway is clear.

- **Promote** recovery: this may be as simple as keeping the patient comfortable until qualified assistance arrives. Reassure and calm the casualty as much as possible.

Key terms

Casualty: the person who has suffered the injury or illness.

Qualified assistance: someone who has a recognised first aid qualification or the emergency services.

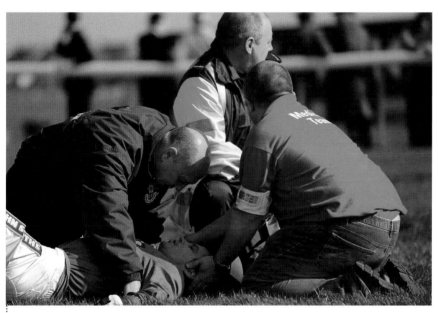

How would you deal with a situation like this?

Skills builder

The way in which you deal with casualties is vitally important as you are likely to be the first person on the scene.

- Ask if you can observe and assist in any first aid incidents.

- Watch how first aid incidents are managed.

- Practise carrying out an initial assessment and relaying this to your supervisor to request qualified assistance.

- Assist your colleagues in protecting the person from initial harm and from any further risk of injury.

- Comfort and reassure the person until you are relieved by a qualified person.

Decide who to contact (on-site first aider or emergency services)

You will not usually need to decide who to contact – this is the role of your supervision/control room via the chain of command. However, in exceptional circumstances (e.g., if you are unable to communicate with your supervisor or control room) you may need to make this decision yourself. Usually this will be a first aider or other qualified person such as an on-site doctor or paramedic. The situation you find yourself in and the seriousness of the patient's injury or illness will determine who you need to contact.

Unit 204 Deal with accidents and emergencies

Always try to contact your supervisor/control room immediately and ask for medical assistance. You will need to inform them of important and immediate details such as:

☐ what happened (including details of any injuries/illness)

☐ why and how the incident occurred

☐ who is involved

☐ where the casualty is (on a large site, the exact location will be required).

Find out if you are able to stay with the injured person to provide casualty management until medical assistance arrives.

In the meantime, you should:

☐ keep yourself, the casualty and the public calm

☐ manage the situation

☐ check to see if there are any hazards or risks that could cause further injury (for example, a fire which had caused a burn injury could be out of control, or the casualty or other people could be close to the fire)

☐ remove or reduce the chance of further injury by organising the removal of any hazards (if possible) and/or moving the casualty and others to a safe place

☐ **never** move the casualty unless they are in real danger of further, serious injury

☐ **never** touch anything at the scene of the incident that may be the cause of the injury (e.g. an offensive weapon) unless there is a real chance of it being used again

☐ if you are considering trying to move a casualty (e.g., if a fire is out of control, or part of a building near to you is in imminent danger of collapse), carry out a dynamic risk assessment of your own personal safety and that of others.

Make sure that your chain of command is fully aware of the situation; inform your supervisors before taking any action and follow instructions carefully and promptly.

Contact your supervisor or control room immediately to ask what you should do if there is an incident

Contact the on-site first aider

All venues will have on-site first aiders and first-aid facilities. These people could be employees of the venue, doctors, paramedics, safety staff, external contractors, or volunteers such as the St John Ambulance Service or British Red Cross.

The number and location of first aiders and first aid resources will depend on the size and nature of the event. You will need to be aware of who and where the qualified first aiders are; their details will be provided during the pre-event briefing.

Always make any requests for a first aider through the chain of command and be clear about the type of casualty, the extent of their injury or illness and their exact location.

Procedures for contacting the emergency services

In the majority of instances all requests to contact the emergency services must be made through the chain of command. However, your risk assessment, the circumstances of the incident and the condition of the casualty might mean that the fastest way to obtain help is to go straight to your control room, or even to ring the emergency services on your mobile phone. It is your decision and your justification will be taken into account in the final report. The number for the emergency services in the UK is 999. You will need to state which of the services you require and explain clearly what the problem is.

Why we need to provide comfort and reassurance

This is a fundamental issue in first aid and in caring for any patient. Keep the patient safe and warm, talk to them and let them know that everything is under control and help is on the way. This will reassure the casualty and reduce stress and shock. Remain calm, no matter how serious the injury or illness appears: this will help the casualty, other people and yourself.

 Remember: Keep calm when involved in casualty management. Your calmness and control will have an immediate effect on everyone around you.

If you are dealing with an injured child, make sure one of their parents or a guardian is present

You might be dealing with children, elderly people or people with particular needs (e.g., disabilities, medical conditions or difficulties in understanding the English language). For example, an injured child or a person with particular requirements may be suffering from a very minor injury such as a sprained wrist after falling down. However, you will need to have the person's parent/guardian/carer with them when they are being treated as part of the reassurance and care that you offer. Remember also that other people involved — colleagues, friends, witnesses or other onlookers — may be shocked or traumatised by the experience and may also need reassurance.

Shock can prevent a quick recovery and will often lead to a patient's condition deteriorating. You can play a very important role while awaiting a qualified first aider or the arrival of the emergency services by providing reassurance and comfort.

How to provide reassurance and comfort

Always keep checking for a response from the casualty when you are talking, and continue to talk and listen to make sure that the patient is as comfortable as possible under the circumstances. Find out everything you can about the injury or illness, so you can inform the control room and the qualified medical assistance on their arrival.

If at any stage you get no response from the patient, slightly shake the person's arm(s) to see if you receive any eye contact, speech or arm movements. Never move an injured person in a way that may cause further injury unless there is a definite risk of further serious harm (e.g., a fire or risk of structural collapse). Do not attempt to move the casualty if there is a risk that you will be harmed in the process.

Give clear and accurate information to the qualified assistance

When the qualified assistance arrives at the scene, it is your responsibility to provide as much information as possible. This will help the first aider or medical professional to understand the situation and decide how to treat the casualty.

If you are able, and you have permission to do so, assist the medically qualified person or first aider if required. Make sure you follow any instructions.

What information should you give the first aider?

 Remember: Obtain as much relevant information as possible about the circumstances of the injury or illness. You could ask the casualty or others at the scene who may have seen what happened. This information is vital for the first aider and will help them to make an early diagnosis and provide the correct treatment.

Accident reporting procedures

All accidents or injuries (no matter how minor) will need to be reported and recorded, whether they involve you, your colleagues, a member of the public or anyone else visiting the venue. There will be organisational and venue procedures to follow in respect of accident reporting, which you will be informed of during the pre-event briefing. You will be told where the forms are and when you should complete the report. You should also make notes in your pocket book during or immediately after any incident to remind you of important information.

Accident reports are used to monitor and analyse the number, type and location of incidents so that further incidents can be prevented in the future. There is also the possibility that people who have been involved in an accident will seek compensation. Your report may be an important part of this process and will be retained by the event organisers for many years.

As soon as possible after an incident, you must return to your original duties and resume your role. However, you should report the incident as soon as possible using detailed notes made at the time the incident occurred.

Figure 204.1 An example of an accident report

Functional skills

English: Writing – Within this learning outcome, you will have shown that you can:

* plan what you need to write (by obtaining information, using your notebook and completing an accident report)

* organise your notebook and report into chronological order

* check your work for grammar, punctuation and spelling errors

* submit the report to your supervisor or line manager.

Your report should be as full and as accurate as possible should contain the following important details:

☐ **who** – the full details of the patient(s) and your full details

☐ **what** – a detailed description of the incident

☐ **where** – the exact location, venue, area position

☐ **why** – any medical information or other evidence that might explain why the incident occurred

☐ **when** – time, day, date

☐ **how** – information from people who witnessed the incident.

RIDDOR

The Health and Safety Executive (HSE) issues guidelines for the reporting of injuries, diseases and dangerous occurrences (such as gas leaks), commonly known as RIDDOR. Reporting incidents is a legal requirement and the HSE and local authorities will carry out investigations into serious accidents. The following incidents need to be reported:

☐ work-related deaths

☐ major injuries which require more than three days off work

☐ work-related diseases

☐ dangerous occurrences or near misses.

Other organisations that could carry out investigations into accidents and incidents are:

☐ the police

☐ the fire service

☐ the local authority

☐ a court of law

☐ a coroner.

Skills builder

Ask if you can be present during a first aid incident to observe how it is managed. Make a note of:

* how the casualty is protected

* how the incident is described to the control room and qualified assistance

* how the casualty is reassured and kept calm and comfortable

* what information and notes are made at the scene and reported in full afterwards.

Best Practice Checklist

Dealing with accidents or emergencies

- Know and understand your role in the emergency procedures.
- The safety, welfare and wellbeing of everyone at the event are a priority. Know how to protect the casualty from harm and the risk of further harm — from people, place and objects.
- Your role during an incident or accident is casualty management — not first aid.
- Contact your supervisor/control room and provide details.
- Remember the three 'P's: **Prevent** further danger, **Preserve** life and **Promote** recovery.
- Keep checking for a response from the casualty.
- By remaining calm, professional and in control you will prevent unnecessary fear and panic.
- Know the main evacuation routes as well as alternative routes.
- Know where the emergency equipment is kept and how to use it.
- Call for qualified assistance whenever required and do not move the casualty.
- Obtain as much information as possible from the casualty or others and make notes.
- Provide as much background information as you can to the qualified first aider to assist in an early diagnosis.
- Report the incident as soon as possible following your procedures.

Follow emergency procedures

Emergency procedures

In your role as an event steward, you may have to deal with the following **emergency** situations:

- fires
- security incidents
- missing people.

Emergency routes and exit points need to be kept clear at all times. You will need to carry out regular checks to confirm that exit routes are clear and gates and doors are not locked. This is part of the event risk assessment.

The main reasons for carrying out pre-event safety checks are:

- to make sure all emergency and safety equipment is working properly
- to make sure you know what equipment is available and where it is located and
- to familiarise you with evacuation routes.

Key term

Emergency: any situation that immediately threatens the health and safety of spectators, staff or yourself (e.g., fires or bomb threats).

 Remember: The prevention and reduction of accidents and incidents is of prime importance and the most important reason for you to carry out safety checks and risk assessments.

Give clear and correct instructions

During an emergency you must give clear and correct instructions so that people understand exactly what you are saying and what they need to do. There must be no confusion or uncertainty as this could lead to indecision and panic. What you say and how you say it could have a direct impact on the survival of the spectators if the emergency escalates.

You also need to remain calm and give people time to take in what you are saying. If necessary, repeat your instructions and look for confirmation that they have been understood. Misunderstandings are likely to lead to further chaos, with a risk of injury or death.

Instructions for different incidents

Your company or the venue where you are working will probably use code words or numbers which denote the level of the emergency situation and the response required. The table below shows an example of the code words that a control room might communicate over the radio, but please note that these will probably differ from venue to venue.

Table 204.2 Examples of codes which could be used for incidents

Alert level	Code words	Repeated	Meaning of Code Words
Red	Charlie team leader contact control	5 times	Evacuate event immediately All other staff to maintain radio silence **Duties** Evacuation as per instructions from chain of command Control and calm public
Yellow	Bravo team leader contact control	3 times	An incident is ongoing Standby for possible partial or full evacuation Status to be changed to red or green within 5 minutes **Duties** Check emergency exits and lighting in your designated area Move obstructions such as barriers Stop vehicles entering (except emergency vehicles) Issue loud hailers
Green	Alpha team leader contact control	3 times	Event is in normal state Any previous alerts are cancelled **Duties** Continue with your duties

Please note that the above is an example only and that this will no doubt be different at your event.

Think about it

You should know what the emergency codes are as soon as they are used.

- Ask for a copy of the emergency codes for the venue where you are working.
- Ask to be involved in a training exercise using the codes as soon as a session is available.

Practise your communication skills so you feel comfortable and confident when addressing crowds

Carry out your role during an emergency calmly and correctly

You should be aware of your role in an emergency through training and the pre-event briefing; however, this might change depending on the severity and circumstances of a serious incident, so you need to listen carefully to instructions. Whatever your role in an emergency, it is essential that you work in a calm and professional manner to provide reassurance, confidence, control and order.

The emergency services may ask you for help, directly or via your supervisor or control room. You must always consider your role and position before agreeing to assist. Depending on the seriousness of the situation, a decision may be required at a higher level.

Skills builder

Working with other members of your team in an emergency situation requires all your teamwork skills and your individual strength to remain calm and controlled.

- Make sure you attend emergency training exercises.

- Involve yourself in the training exercises as realistically as possible.

- Carry out your safety checks carefully and seriously.

- Make notes about your role and the part you will be expected to play in a real emergency.

Case study

You have received instructions that your designated area needs to be evacuated due to a crowd surge, which has resulted in some people being injured. Your role is to make sure that a set of doors at the top of a staircase remains open, as spectators in that area need to leave through these doors. During the evacuation you are asked by a senior fire officer to assist with the removal of casualties who cannot walk, so that they can get to the ambulances waiting at the rear of the stadium.

Over to you

- How will you deal with the request to help injured people?

- What is your priority – your role at the set of doors or the removal of casualties?

- What might happen if 'your' doors are closed during the evacuation because you decided to leave your post?

Don't forget that the decision will need to be made by the chain of command. A senior fire officer is also part of the management chain, but should be made aware that you need to communicate the request to your supervisor/controller.

You will need to know how to deal with the types of incident shown in Table 204.3.

	What problems could occur?	What do you need to do?	What do you need to say?
Fire	• Firefighting equipment failure due to damage or malfunction. • Poor communication or misunderstanding of procedures. • Lack of training. • Fire may spread if not dealt with quickly. • Structural damage. • People may panic, leading to injury and/or death. • People may be reluctant to leave the event, which could delay the evacuation. • People who have been evacuated may try to re-enter the event. • People may congregate near the exits, preventing the emergency services from reaching the scene. • Major crush injuries and death from burning or falling or objects. • Business continuity will be disrupted.	• Know the evacuation routes and plans. • Know where the emergency facilities are. • Know the location of rendezvous points (RV points) in your area. • Know the alternative escape routes in you area. • Remain calm and professional. • Carry out dynamic risk assessments. • Remove people from the fire. • Report the incident immediately. • Restrict entry. • Follow procedures and contingency plans. • Attend regular training events.	• Listen to me. • Keep calm. • Do exactly as I say from now on.

Table 204.3 Examples of incidents and potential problems

Table 204.3 Examples of incidents and potential problems (cont.)

	What problems could occur?	What do you need to do?	What do you need to say?
Security incident	• This will depend on the type of incident, for example: • a suspect package, bomb or terrorist attack • communication loss • fire or gas • biological, chemical, radiological or nuclear incidents • rioting, fighting or criminal damage • crowd problems such as surging, crushing or pitch invasion • delays to the start of an event or late arrivals • theft, burglary or robbery.	• Know the evacuation routes and plans. • Know where the emergency facilities are. • Know the location of rendezvous points (RV points) in your area. • Know the alternative escape routes in you area. • Remain calm and professional. • Remember all necessary search procedures. • Carry out dynamic risk assessments. • Remember your conflict management skills if necessary. • Follow procedures and contingency plans. • Remove people from the area. • Report the incident immediately. • Restrict entry – protect people from harm or further injury and preserve the scene. • Remember, you are not a security officer and a criminal investigation will take place later. • Attend regular training events. • **Remember: safety takes priority over security.**	• Listen to me. • Keep calm. • Do exactly as I say from now on.

Missing persons	• Who has gone missing?
	  ○ Adult or child, male or female, how old?
	  ○ Do they have any particular issues, such as dementia?
	  ○ Has the missing person been using alcohol or drugs?
	• Why has the person gone missing?
	  ○ Did they wander off and get lost?
	  ○ Did they leave for a reason?
	  ○ Could they have been abducted?
	• How long has the person been missing?
		• Remain calm and professional.
		• Obtain a full description and report ASAP.
		• Keep relatives/friends together in the area and conduct a brief search.
		• Brief chain of command for team searches if necessary.
			• Keep calm.
			• Provide a full description to your supervisor or to the control room as soon as possible.

Facilities	• Safety equipment failure due to damage or malfunction. • Major structural damage. • Loss of services (e.g., power cuts will affect lifts, escalators etc.) • Gas or chemical leaks. • Equipment failure (e.g., CCTV, public address systems, telephones and radios, turnstiles etc.). • Problems with fire alarms and fire safety systems. • Failure of lighting or sound systems. • Adverse/severe weather conditions.	• Know the evacuation routes and plans. • Know where the emergency facilities and reserve equipment are. • Know the location of rendezvous points (RV points) in your area. • Know the alternative escape routes in you area. • Remain calm and professional. • Carry out dynamic risk assessments. • Remember your conflict management skills if necessary. • Follow procedures and contingency plans. • Remove people from the area. • Report the incident immediately. • Restrict entry. • Attend regular training events in the use of safety equipment.	

Be aware that there may also be communication barriers. The scene could be chaotic and noisy and you may not be the only person giving instructions, so people may struggle to see and hear you.

A communication barrier is anything that prevents a message being sent (encoded) or received (decoded) so that it can be clearly understood. A risk assessment should be carried out prior to the event to rectify any potential problems of this kind. Ways to reduce crowd noise for stewards include providing those using radios with earpieces and speakers, or installing loud speakers around the grounds.

How would you go about getting this crowd into a manageable queue?

Functional skills

English: Speaking, listening and communication – presenting information clearly and using appropriate language; receiving, listening to and understanding information; and communicating information accurately and clearly to your supervisor or control room will all help develop your English speaking, listening and communication skills.

Think about it

How could you deal with the following blocks to communication, which may prevent your instructions from being understood?

- People may be unable to hear because of noise from those around them or the incident.
- People may not be sure who they should be listening to.
- Stress and panic may make it difficult for people to understand you.
- People may misunderstand directions, e.g. 'my left' will be 'your right' if you are facing me.

Best Practice Checklist

Your role in emergency procedures

☐ Know what your roles and responsibilities are in an emergency but be prepared to change if instructed to do so.

☐ Pre-event safety checks can prevent or minimise the chance of an emergency incident taking place. Carry out regular checks of safety equipment and exit routes.

☐ Be clear, concise and direct when telling people what they need to do: if you confuse people, this may lead to indecision and panic.

☐ Repeat your instructions if necessary, to make sure that people understand: look for visual confirmation that your instructions have been understood.

☐ Always be aware of communication barriers.

☐ Get everyone to do what you want them to do, quickly but calmly.

☐ Be prepare to assist the emergency services if instructed by your chain of command.

Follow correct emergency reporting procedures

Your organisation will have specific procedures for reporting an emergency incident. The procedures will be provided to you at the briefing and will be in your steward's handbook and notes that you take during the briefing.

Your role will be to report an emergency incident to your supervisor/control room as soon as possible so that emergency resources and services can be notified.

Report problems with the emergency procedures

After an emergency procedure has been carried out (including emergency procedure exercises) there will be a full debrief meeting involving all people involved. If you experienced any problems with the procedure, these should be reported to your supervisor without delay so that the problems can be discussed and resolved as soon as possible. In some cases this may even mean a change in the procedure is required, depending upon the circumstances.

Some of the problems with emergency procedures might include:

☐ lack of communication within the chain of command

☐ communication not reaching all event stewards

☐ stewards and the public not grasping the seriousness of the incident

☐ lack of control or management of the evacuation

- public attempting to leave the venue the same way they entered
- lack of communication causing confusion, with people going in different directions
- panic (often through lack of control) causing stampede
- exit gates become overcrowded, causing crushing and injuries.

Skills builder

Being able to report problems at a debrief meeting with your managers and other colleagues requires confidence. You will need to be accurate and concise when speaking.

- Report all relevant problems so that the team does not make the same mistakes again.

- Provide a clear and accurate account of the problem.

- If possible, explain the circumstances which created the problem.

- If you can, suggest ways to prevent the problem from recurring.

Debriefing sessions can be used to identify problems with emergency procedures so they can be avoided next time

Chain of command for managers during emergencies and evacuations

The safety plan for the venue will include the need for a 'graduated response', using its own personnel and resources as the first level of response. However, the level may quickly escalate: if there is an explosion and numerous casualties the graduated response level may need to include the emergency services. The following officers may all be involved in an emergency situation or evacuation:

Safety officer — will authorise the evacuation. The SO is also responsible for requesting the emergency services, instructing the chief steward to ensure that all staff are informed and in position, and working with the emergency services to manage the evacuation.

Senior police officer — will take overall management of an event during a major incident such as an evacuation, and will instruct police. The SPO may bring in additional resources to assist with the evacuation, closing local roads and public transport, if necessary.

Deputy safety officer/chief steward – will work closely with the safety officer and senior police officers to ensure the partnership between the police and stewards is working effectively, and will be responsible for coordinating and managing stewarding activities. The chief steward will also pay particular attention to overcrowding at exits and, if required, identify additional areas which could be used for crowd-holding purposes.

Controllers/radio operators and public address supervisors/stewards/fire marshals/facilities staff – Everyone involved in the event-safety management structure will receive instructions on their respective roles and responsibilities in an emergency, depending on the level of response required. This is referred to as the 'graduated response level'; the level required will be determined by safety officers and other safety managers.

The emergency services will always be consulted and involved in the production of any contingency plan and in training exercises at the venue; they will know what their roles and responsibilities are and how these work together with the team at the venue, including event stewards.

The roles and responsibilities of the emergency services can be summarised as shown in Table 204.4.

Emergency service	Roles and responsibilities
Police	Road closures, traffic control, access and exit control, crowd control, security and emergency evacuation planning, management of crime and disorder, casualty identification, scenes of crime, forensic investigations
Fire	Fire safety advice, management of fire hazards, emergency and evacuation planning, firework displays and bonfires, life saving, rescue services, firefighting, casualty management, investigation into fires (including forensic investigations)
Medical services	(e.g. St John Ambulance, St Andrew's First Aid, British Red Cross, The NHS Ambulance Service) On-site provision, paramedics, doctors, first aid facilities, life-saving emergency care, treatment and medicines for seriously ill or injured people, transportation to hospitals
NHS hospitals	Involved in contingency planning for large events and in receiving casualties from major incidents

Table 204.4 Roles and responsibilities of the emergency services

 Remember: Relatively minor issues can soon escalate into major incidents unless there is a process in place to ensure that hazards are identified and dealt with effectively.

Best Practice Checklist

Following emergency procedures

☐ Learn the emergency code words and what they mean.

☐ Get involved in as many training exercises as you can – it's the best way to learn how to deal with emergencies.

☐ Act professionally at all times.

☐ Learn how to give clear, concise and simple instructions.

☐ Make sure that you have been heard and understood; look for confirmation.

☐ Know where the escape routes are and check them regularly.

☐ If possible find out where there are alternative escape routes.

☐ Know where the emergency equipment is and learn how to use it.

☐ Learn how, and who to report emergencies to.

☐ Be confident and professional when reporting any problems with emergency procedures.

☐ Identifying, reviewing and monitoring procedures enables organisations to learn lessons from mistakes or correct procedures before they happen.

☐ Rectify any problems as soon as possible.

Working Life

Tara's story

I work as event steward once a year at a large open-air music festival; it's usually pretty muddy and people are always slipping and hurting themselves. Last year I saw someone burn themselves on an open fire. He was in agony and in too much pain to travel far. I informed my supervisor and the control room by radio of what had happened, and then did everything I could to protect the person from further injury, keeping him calm and reassuring him he would be OK.

The fire looked like it could easily get out of control, so we slowly moved away and I instructed others to put it out. While waiting for the qualified assistance I took notes about what had happened, details of the casualty and witnesses.

Help arrived a few minutes later and the casualty was taken to the local hospital for treatment. I informed my supervisor/control and continued with my job. Later I completed an accident report and submitted it through my supervisor.

Ask the expert

Q If I'm not sure whether I should try to move a casualty or not – what should I do?

A Generally, you should never try to move an injured person as this might cause further injury. However, if there is an immediate danger which could cause further injury (such as a spreading fire, or a structure about to collapse), you must carry out a dynamic risk assessment based on your own safety and that of others, and make a decision.

Q I'm not very good at reading, especially large documents; how can I learn about the evacuation procedures at my venue?

A The best way to learn is to practise and watch experienced people. Make sure you know your role in an emergency and note any important points. Attend training sessions and evacuation exercises and talk to experienced colleagues and your supervisor about emergency procedures.

Top tips

- ✔ When you manage casualties, always act calmly and professionally.

- ✔ Protect the casualty and others from risk of further injury.

- ✔ Make notes, collecting as much information as possible for the accident report form.

Unit 204 Deal with accidents and emergencies

Check your knowledge

1 Why is it important that accidents and emergencies are dealt with promptly, calmly and correctly?
a) to prevent any further danger
b) to prevent panic
c) to preserve life and promote recovery
d) all of the above.

2 How would you deal with injuries or illnesses before qualified assistance arrives?

3 How do you decide whether to contact the on-site first aider or immediately call the emergency services?

4 Why is it important to protect the casualty (and others involved) from harm?

5 Why is it important to provide comfort and reassurance and how would you do so?

6 What is the procedure for reporting accidents?

7 How do you report problems with the emergency procedures?

8 Why should you give clear, accurate and simple instructions?
a) so that everyone can discuss them
b) so that everyone can write them down
c) so that they can be repeated easily and everyone understands what they need to do to be safe
d) so that your performance can be assessed.

9 What actions do you need to take if a child is reported missing to you?

10 How do you know about the content of the emergency procedures and what your specific role is?

Getting ready for assessment

Once you have had some experience of and feel confident when dealing with accidents and injuries, you will be ready to be assessed towards this unit.

You will have to prove you are able to remain calm, follow your organisation's procedures while protecting casualties and others from further risk, know how and when to call for assistance and comfort and reassure the people involved.

It is also important that you collect as much information as possible for the qualified assistance and complete a written record.

Check your knowledge answers

Unit 203 How stewards prepare for spectator events

1 Answers can include:

- entertainment licence
- premises licence
- temporary events notice
- insurance cover
- risk assessment
- the Health and Safety at Work Act 1974
- the Safety of Sports Grounds Act 1975
- Fire Safety and Places of Sports Act 1987
- the Sporting Events (Control of Alcohol etc) Act 1985
- noise control (Environmental Protection Act)
- street collection permit
- road closure order and temporary orders
- street trading licence.

2 You should attend the pre-event briefing so that you know what you are required to do. At the briefing the steward will be given:

- their role and responsibilities at that event
- information and intelligence about the crowd and what to expect.

The information which is provided is 'need to know' and 'nice to know'. Both are important.

3 1 sign in/registration

2 collect uniform

3 collect equipment (radio, torch etc.)

4 attend briefing with supervisor or manager

5 conduct sweep of venue for hazards/risks

6 take position before customer entry.

4. Look for key phrases in the answer such as:

- quickly and easily recognise that you are a steward
- because people will need to find help if there is an incident
- because people will need to know who to approach to seek an answer to a problem
- so you are quickly recognisable by your colleagues as well as the emergency services. If an emergency occurs it is important that your colleagues can identify you so that the incident can be managed and controlled properly.
- so that the event managers know you are a trained steward who is authorised to be at that event.

5.
- Safety equipment such as a fire extinguisher or your high visibility jacket:

  Obvious damage to the equipment such as a broken nozzle.

  Ripped or dirty jacket.
- Security equipment such as a locked exit gate:
  A lock on a gate which should be unlocked when customers enter the premises is still locked.
- Emergency equipment such as a fire emergency exit sign:
  The bulb is broken so the exit sign will not illuminate.

6. Stewards conduct a pre-event check to ensure a safe environment for everyone at the event: you, the public and staff.

7. The three 'R's
- restrict access to the hazard
- remove the hazard if possible
- report the hazard to your supervisor.

8. The three signs are: 'No Smoking', 'Fire Exit Keep Clear', 'Now wash your hands please'.

9.
- confined areas:
  too many people entering the area
- open areas:
  weather conditions, open fires
- public areas:
  slips, trips and falls
- non-public areas:
  noise, electrical cabling

10
- potential hazards and risks
- stewarding procedures
- venue rules.

Unit 205 Control the entry, exit and movement of people at spectator events

1 It is important to wear the correct identification so that you are easily identifiable and people know who to ask for information.

2 A poorly managed queue might result in surging, conflicts arising, loss of control, injury, possible illegal entry to the venue.

3 You should clearly and politely explain to someone why you are refusing them entry so they understand why and you can avoid potential conflict.

4 You should monitor your designated area carefully to ensure the safety of the public and your colleagues at all times.

5 You must only search people of the same sex as yourself because it is the event policy and organisational procedure.

6 You should ask their permission, only search outer garments and search from top to toe.

7 You should provide people with courtesy and proper explanations because it de-escalates the potential for conflict and is a good customer care principle.

8 With all of these people you should be professional at all times and apply appropriate communication and conflict management skills.

9 You should try to get all the relevant information because you need the full picture to make informed decisions.

10 You should refer problems to a colleague, your supervisor or control room, or an information point.

Unit 206 Monitor spectators and deal with crowd problems

[1] There are different types of problems that can occur within a crowd and in your designated area. A steward is the first line of sight because they are in a position to be able to see and hear what is happening, talk to spectators about potential problems and report issues before they happen. Stewards are therefore part of the 'dynamic risk assessment'.

[2] You should observe the behaviour of individuals and the crowd. Look for signs of sudden or unexpected crowd movement, overcrowding in your designated area or in the venue, people who look distressed or unwell, people who appear to be separated from the group, unlawful behaviour, unsociable behaviour, and people moving into restricted areas.

[3] A steward should always act in a professional manner, being polite, courteous and helpful to all spectators regardless of their affiliations. Being impartial means that you do not favour anyone when making a decision. It means that you will act fairly when dealing with everyone, acting at all times in good faith, making honest, impartial decisions with integrity.

[4] **Confined areas**

Possible answers include:

- too many people in a small area at the same time
- overcrowding in a confined room or staircase
- everyone trying to get to the bar or toilets at the same time.

Open areas

Possible answers include:

- mix of different crowd types
- moving in the area freely
- people standing
- crowds coming in from two different directions
- potential problems with crowd density
- weather conditions can impact on crowd behaviour
- sudden heavy rain, thunder or lightning can cause people to run for cover.

Public areas

Possible examples include:

- areas can be unticketed, so you may have no idea how many people to expect
- overcrowding on the pavement
- jostling, which can lead to people being forced into the path of an oncoming vehicle
- spectators becoming argumentative and potentially aggressive due to being pushed or jostled
- children running into the street
- drunken spectators (a danger to themselves and others)
- damage to buildings or scaffolding as a result of people climbing to get a better view
- rubbish in the street or rubbish bins which are hazards and provide possible missiles to throw at people/procession.

5 It is very important that stewards remain:

- alert
- calm
- controlled
- polite
- courteous
- helpful
- well trained
- professional
- impartial to everyone
- attentive to individual needs and to the crowd.

6 There are many types of crowd problems for example, overcrowding, fighting and unsociable behaviour; the procedures to follow will be agreed and written down. All actions should be taken as soon as possible after the problem has been identified. An early response to an actual or potential problem should always be to:

- seek assistance and report the problem immediately
- remain alert, calm and professional
- report the problem clearly and ask for help to deal with it
- focus on your roles and responsibilities, remaining customer-focused
- reassure people around you
- assess the risk before you take any action.

7. During an incident or an emergency it is vital to encourage people to be calm and to reassure people around you because it prevents panic from spreading. If they see you acting in a professional, calm way, people will respond in a similar manner.

8. Possible answers include:

   - acting irresponsibly
   - ignoring risk assessments
   - ignoring procedures
   - not following instructions
   - not reporting a potential or actual problem
   - panicking, instead of acting calmly and professionally.

9. Assessment involves:

   - gathering all the necessary information in relation to a crowd problem and working out the level of risk to yourself and others
   - looking at the behaviour of the crowd and making a decision as to whether a problem or incident needs to be dealt with immediately, deferred, or not dealt with at all
   - reporting the evaluation of the risk to the supervisor.

   The issues being monitored in that crowd will be based upon density, dynamics and distress. The risk assessment you are carrying out as you observe the crowd is a balance of the likelihood that something will happen against the severity of injury that may occur.

10. Communicating with people is always a priority as this will provide everyone involved, including colleagues, with information. Accurate and clear information helps the decision on what level of support or resources are required to deal with an incident. Your attitude and behaviour must be professional. Clear and assertive communication is also required when dealing with an incident; people need to know exactly what is expected of them and what will happen in the event of non-compliance. The key is to establish order, to get people's attention as quickly as possible and avoid an escalation of the problem. On these occasions people are looking for an answer to a problem and will often look for a leader who is able to offer a solution.

Unit 201 Help to manage conflict

1. The most important legal consideration is that the force used must be 'reasonable and justifiable in the circumstances'.

2 If everyone understands what is happening and why, you are more likely to succeed in defusing the situation.

3 Our personal space is the space we like to maintain during our normal working or daily relationships with the people we know.

4 Active listening improves understanding and relationships between people.

5 Empathy confirms understanding and builds trust.

6 It is important to keep key people informed so that they can provide advice and assistance.

7 In case of legal action, it is important to have a clear and detailed account of what happened.

8 An authentic report should have been written by you and signed and dated as soon as it was complete.

9 Answers may include:

- documentary evidence such as an incident report
- photographic evidence such as a digital recording
- physical evidence such as a weapon.

10 Words – 7%, tone of voice – 38%, **non-verbal communication – 55%**

Research has shown that the strongest message a person receives via any spoken communication is likely to come from non-verbal clues (body language) of the person who is speaking.

Unit 202 Contribute to the work of the team

1 You will find details in British Standard (BS 8406:2009) Event stewarding and crowd safety: Code of Practice, as well as in your organisation's policies and procedures.

2 **d** It ensures high-quality and professional standards for individuals, the team and the company.

3 An effective working relationship is one that helps the team to work well and provide a high level of service to the customer. This includes getting along well with your colleagues, being fair to them, avoiding unnecessary disagreements and not letting your personal life influence the way you relate to colleagues.

4 Make an effort to get to know each other professionally, be fair, open and honest, and learn each other's strengths and weaknesses.

5 **b** through the chain of command.

6 If you do not or cannot perform your role effectively, this could affect public safety. You will also make life more difficult for your colleagues, since they may have to do your job for you.

7 You may need to ask for help in a potential conflict situation, if you encounter a situation you are not qualified to deal with, or if there is an emergency and you need the help of others to decide on the correct course of action. An event steward should never be afraid to ask for help, especially when there are risks. The chain of command should always be involved.

8 An event steward should always provide help and information unless it is illegal or inappropriate to do so (for example, if someone asks you to perform a task you are not licensed to do, such as searching people, guarding or ejecting spectators from a venue).

9 You will become an effective member of the team by contributing and adding suggestions and information, listening to and taking note of information and reviewing what has happened.

10 Customer feedback is key to improving customer service skills, for your own development, the team's development and the company's development.

Unit 204 Deal with accidents and emergencies

1 **d** all of the above.

2 Before qualified assistance arrives you should deal with accidents and emergencies by remembering the letters DRABC, protect the casualty, preserve life and promote recovery.

3 | It's not your decision. Your role is to report the facts immediately through your chain of command after you have assessed the situation. Based on your assessment, you might make a recommendation but you would not make the decision.

4 | The casualty (and others involved) should be protected to prevent risk of further harm and injury.

5 | It is important to provide comfort and reassurance because it promotes recovery. If possible, cover the person with a coat to retain body heat as they may be in shock. Talk to the person and provide reassurance until qualified assistance arrives.

6 | The procedure for reporting accidents is to inform your supervisor/control room immediately and keep notes relating to the circumstances of the incident, the casualty and any witnesses.

7 | Any problems with the emergency procedures should be reported through the chain of command and at the debrief.

8 | **c** so that they can be repeated easily and everyone understands what they need to do to be safe.

9 | If a child is reported missing, keep calm and try to keep everyone else calm. Provide a full description to supervisor/control room as soon as possible, ask family or friends to search the immediate area and come back to you.

10 | The content of the emergency procedures and specific roles within them will be given at the briefing and the handbook will contain details. Details can also be written down in a notebook during the briefing.

Useful resources

Crowd management and other organisations

The Association of Event Organisers http://www.aeo.org.uk/

Centre for Crowd Management and Security Studies, Bucks New University, http://www.crowdsafetymanagement.co.uk/

The Football League, Security and Operations Adviser, t. 0870 442 9221 www.fl@football-league.co.uk

Football Licensing Authority, t. 020 7930 6693 www.flaweb.org.uk/fla

Football Safety Officers Association Ltd. (F.S.O.A.), t. 01773 520606 www.fsoa.org.uk

Health and Safety Executive, http://www.hse.gov.uk/

The Journal of Crowd Safety and Security Management - An Online Journal, http://www.crowdsafetymanagement.co.uk/journal

NaCTSO (National Counter Terrorism Security Office), t. 020 7931 7142 www.nactso.gov.uk

National Outdoor Events Association, http://noea.org.uk/

Royal Society for the Prevention of Accidents www.rospa.com

Safe Concerts, http://www.safeconcerts.com/crowdsafety/

UK Sport www.uksport.gov.uk

United Kingdom Crowd Management Association (UKCMA) http://www.ukcma.com/

Standard-setting bodies and organisations

The Security Industry Authority, http://www.sia.homeoffice.gov.uk/pages/home.aspx

SkillsActive, National Occupational Standards, http://www.skillsactive.com/training/standards

Skills for Security the skills body for the security industry, http://www.skillsforsecurity.org.uk/

Awarding bodies

City & Guilds, http://www.cityandguilds.com/

Edexcel, http://www.edexcel.com/

NCFE, http://www.ncfe.org.uk

Textbooks

Frosdick S et al — *Safety and Security at Sports Grounds* (Paragon, 2005) ISBN 1899820167

Related reports and publications

The Event Safety Guide (HSE, 1999) (Purple Guide)

Counter Terrorism Protective Security Advice for Stadia and Arenas (NaCTSO)

Guide to Safety at Sports Grounds 5th Edition (Department for culture, media and sport, 2008) (Green Guide)

Lord Justice Taylor Report into the Hillsborough Stadium Disaster (HMSO, 1990)

Managing Crowds Safely in Public Venues, 2nd Edition (HMSO,2000)

Northern Ireland Guide to Safety at Sports Grounds (Red Guide) Department of Culture, Arts and Leisure, 2007)

Security at Events; Guidance on the Private Security Industry Act 2001 (Security Industry Authority 2008)

Related reports and publications to refer to 'The Popplewell Inquiry' (Hansard 1985) which is the Bradford City FC Fire Disaster

British Standard (BS 8406: 2009) Event stewarding and crowd safety: Code of Practice

Journals

Occupational Safety and Health Journal (RoSPA)

Popular large events in the UK

Bestival

The Big Chill

Bridgwater Carnival

Download

Edinburgh Festival

Glastonbury Festival

Henley Royal Regatta

Isle of Wight Festival

Latitude Festival

Leeds Festival

London 2012 Olympic and Paralympic Games

Notting Hill Carnival

Reading Festival

V Festival

Glossary

Active listening — showing that you are paying attention to what someone is saying, for example, by maintaining eye contact, nodding, asking further questions.

Appearance — this includes wearing the correct clothes, presenting a professional image and having the correct identification.

Assess — gather all necessary information relating to a crowd problem and work out the level of risk to yourself and others

Body language — the showing of feelings by the way someone moves or holds their body.

Casualty — the person who has suffered the injury or illness.

Colleagues — the people you work with (those working at your own level and your managers).

Communicate — by using words, as well as body language, tone of voice, etc.

Communications resources — these resources could be notebooks for recording incidents, or communications equipment such as radios, if appropriate.

Conflict — situations in which people disagree strongly, which may lead to violence or other forms of unlawful or unsociable behaviour.

Debrief — feeding back information relating to the way the event was managed and any incidents that occurred.

Designated area — the area you are responsible for.

Discrimination — the unfair treatment of a person or a group, on the basis of prejudice.

Diversity — is about valuing everyone as an individual. People are not alike, and everyone has their own tastes, needs, personality, culture, beliefs and behaviours.

Emergency — any situation that immediately threatens the health and safety of spectators, staff or yourself (for example, fires or bomb threats).

Emergency services — usually the fire service, ambulance service or police.

Equality — is when everyone is treated equally, regardless of their differences in age, gender, race, religion or belief, ethnic origin, sexual orientation, gender reassignment and disability.

Evaluation — thinking about your work and identifying what you do well and how you could improve.

Event — any type of public event (for example a sporting event or musical performance).

Feedback – comments from other people (customers or colleagues) telling you what they think.

Future responsibilities – these could be new duties that you want to take on or new duties that your line manager wants to give you. This could include promotion.

Hazard – anything with the potential to cause harm (e.g. electricity, hazardous substances, excessive noise).

Hygiene hazard – anything causing a risk to hygiene, for example, unsanitary toilets.

Hyperthermia – excessive increase in body temperature.

Hypothermia – excessive reduction in body temperature.

Impartial – not favouring or discriminating against any particular type of person.

Licensable activity – a licensable activity is determined by the role that is performed and the activity undertaken. These are described fully in Section 3 and Schedule 2 of the Private Security Industry Act 2001 (as amended).

Monitoring – keeping a careful eye on a situation.

Particular needs – the needs, for example, of disabled people, elderly people or children.

Personal space – the amount of space a person needs around them in order to feel comfortable. Getting too close to someone – invading their personal space – is likely to make a difficult situation worse.

Policies – what an organisation says its staff should and should not do in certain situations.

Procedures – a way of carrying out policies as part of an activity or process.

Prejudice – a strong belief, opinion or judgement made without finding out the facts.

Prohibited items – items not allowed into venues under any circumstances.

Qualified assistance – someone who has a recognised first aid qualification or the emergency services.

Resources – the equipment you need to help you in your duties.

Risk – the likelihood of a hazard causing harm and the seriousness of this harm.

Sensitive questioning – asking questions in a way that is not going to make the situation worse, for example, by being polite and phrasing questions so as not to upset someone.

Spectator event – this could be any type of public event or performance, including sporting.

Suspect items – any item which arouses suspicion, such as an unattended bag or package.

Tannoy system — a public address system usually in the form of a series of loudspeakers positioned around the ground, so that important messages can be relayed to visitors and staff at an event.

Team discussions — these will usually be team meetings but could include more informal discussions with team members and line managers.

Training and development — this could involve a course, watching other members of staff doing things that are new to you and receiving instructions from them, or having the opportunity to practise new skills.

Unauthorised entrance — an entrance that has not been approved.

Venue — the grounds or building where an event takes place.

Vomitory — an entrance or exit at any level of a stadium, leading to the seating areas and providing access to other parts of the stadium.

Working relationship — the type of relationship with your colleagues that will help the team to work well and provide a high level of service to the customer; this includes getting along well with your colleagues, being fair to them, avoiding unnecessary disagreements and not letting your personal life influence the way you relate to colleagues.

Index

Key terms are indicated by **bold** page numbers.